What's for Dinner in the Northwest?

Dinner Menus
Featuring Northwest Foods

by

Maryana Vollstedt
The Cookbook Factory
P.O. Box 11515
Eugene, Oregon 97440-3715

1

ISBN 0-910983-14-3
Special acknowledgement: Peter Bang-Knudsen
Advisor: Patty Blickenstaff
Wine & cheese consultants: Roger and Karen Rutan, of Grape and Grain
Cover and title pages by: Marv Boggs
Typesetting by: Ad Type and Stats
Printed by: Shelton Turnbull Printers

INTRODUCTION

One of the advantages of living in the Northwest (besides the beautiful scenery, mild climate, friendly people and varied activities) is the abundance of fresh seasonal foods.

There is a constant supply of seafood and fish available at different times of the year. The Northwest is famous for its salmon, halibut, shellfish, trawlfish, steelhead and trout.

Fishing plays an important role in the economy of the Northwest. It is also a popular recreational sport attracting many fishing enthusiasts to the area.

The Northwest is one of the most fertile growing areas in the nation producing the finest quality fruit, vegetables, grains and nuts. Many of these products are shipped to other parts of the United States and exported to other countries. Fresh produce can always be found in local markets or fruit and vegetable stands. One of the oldest and largest continuously operating public markets in the country is the well known Pike Place Market located in Seattle. Shoppers and tourists come to this historical district where there are stalls and shops of beautifully displayed fresh produce, seafood and specialty foods.

For many years the Northwest has been a source of premium beef, poultry, pork and lamb. All the meats are readily available to local consumers. Another top ranking industry in the Northwest is the production of dairy products. Several cheese factories have gained a national reputation and extensive distribution of their outstanding cheeses.

The production of wine is a relatively new and growing business in the Northwest. Many fine quality wines have been developed which are making an impact on the wine market. Also popular are the premium Northwest beers made from locally grown hops and barley.

For the recreational hunter, deer, elk, pheasant, duck and other wild birds can be found in remote areas. This seasonably available wild game adds variety to the Northwest menu.

In this book the recipes focus on a Northwest cuisine that is developing from the abundant fresh ingredients available and the lifestyle of the people in the Northwest. The menus fit the season as well as the occasion. For good cooking and healthful eating, enjoy "What's for Dinner in the Northwest."

TABLE OF CONTENTS

Fruits, vegetables, cheese and wine included in all sections.

Seafood and Fish

Canal Shrimp Stroganoff

Parslied Rice

Fresh Asparagus

Butter Lettuce and Pine Nut Salad

Frozen Raspberry Pie

Oregon Sauvignon Blanc

CANAL SHRIMP STROGANOFF

*1½-2 lbs. shrimp, cleaned and
  shelled (4-6 shrimp per person
  depending on size)*
6 Tbs. butter, divided
2 cups sliced mushrooms
3 Tbs. minced green onions
1 clove garlic, minced
3 Tbs. flour

1½ cups chicken stock
¼ cup white wine
1 tsp. prepared mustard
1 cup sour cream
1 tsp. dill weed
¼ tsp. salt
Freshly grated pepper

Saute shrimp in 3 Tbs. butter until pink (3-5 minutes). Remove and keep warm. Melt remaining butter in same pan and saute mushrooms, onions and garlic 2 minutes. Add flour and blend. Add stock, wine and mustard and stir-cook until thickened.* Remove from heat and blend in sour cream, dill, salt and pepper. Return to heat and add shrimp. Reheat but do not boil. Serve over long grain or wild rice. Serves 6.

* Can be made ahead to this point.

BUTTER LETTUCE and PINE NUT SALAD

1-2 heads butter lettuce, torn　　*1 avocado, sliced*
¼ cup pine nuts

Combine with Lemon-Dill Dressing (page 47). Use only enough dressing to moisten.

FROZEN RASPBERRY PIE

2 cups fresh raspberries　　　　*1 cup whipping cream, whipped*
1 cup sugar　　　　　　　　　　*¼ cup chopped toasted almonds*
2 egg whites (room temperature)　*Baked 9-inch pie shell or graham*
1 Tbs. lemon juice　　　　　　　* cracker crust*

Combine berries, sugar, egg whites and lemon juice. Beat 15 minutes at high speed until stiff. Fold in whipped cream and almonds. Mound in pie shell. Freeze until serving time.

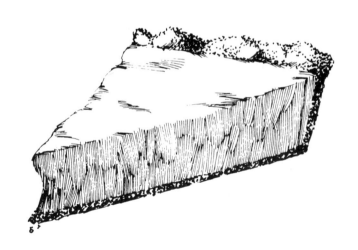

STUFFED MUSHROOMS

16 large mushroom caps,
   uniform size
3-3½ Tbs. butter
1 clove garlic
¼ cup chopped onions

½ cup fine bread crumbs
1 Tbs. Parmesan cheese
¼ tsp. salt
⅛ tsp. oregano
1 Tbs. chopped parsley

Remove stems from mushrooms and chop. Cook with garlic and onions in butter. Add crumbs, Parmesan cheese, salt, oregano and parsley. Place caps on a baking sheet stem side up. Add filling. Bake 10 minutes at 350°.

SEAFOOD AU GRATIN

6 fillets of sole
¾ lb. scallops, cut up if large
1 lb. small cooked shrimp
¾ lb. crab

1½ cups jack cheese, grated
2 batches hollandaise sauce
Fine dried bread crumbs
Paprika and minced parsley

Lightly butter individual casseroles or au gratins. Place fillets on bottom and layer with scallops, shrimp and crab. Top with cheese. Cover with hollandaise and sprinkle lightly with bread crumbs. Bake 10-15 minutes at 425° until bubbly. Watch carefully as it will burn. Top should be slightly browned. Sprinkle with paprika and parsley. Serves 6.

Hollandaise Sauce:

3 egg yolks
2 Tbs. lemon juice
Dash cayenne

¼ tsp. salt
½ cup butter, heated to bubbling
but not browned

Place yolks, lemon juice, cayenne and salt in blender or food processor and blend for 3 seconds. Pour butter into egg mixture in a slow, steady stream, blending until thick and fluffy (about 30 seconds).

BARLEY-RICE PILAF

¼ cup butter
¼ cup chopped almonds
1 onion, chopped
1 clove garlic, minced
2/3 cup brown rice
1/3 cup barley, washed

2 cups beef broth
¼ cup white wine
¼ tsp. each basil, oregano and salt
Freshly ground pepper
¼ cup chopped parsley

Stir nuts in butter until lightly browned. Add onion and garlic and cook until slightly limp. Add rice and barley and stir. Add broth, wine, seasonings and parsley. Bring to boil and reduce heat to simmer. Cover and cook about 45 minutes.

ROMAINE-BACON SALAD

1 head romaine, leaves separated
½ cup freshly grated Romano
cheese

6 slices bacon, cooked and
crumbled
3 eggs, hard-cooked and grated

Place leaves on plate. Top with cheese, bacon and eggs. Drizzle dressing over.

Dressing:

¾ cup oil
¼ cup red wine vinegar
1 tsp. salt
1 tsp. dry mustard

¼ tsp. pepper
½ tsp. basil
1 tsp. lemon juice

Combine all ingredients and chill. Makes enough for 2 salads.

Variation:

ROMAINE-BACON APPLE SALAD

Tear romaine into bite size pieces. Omit eggs and add 1 sliced apple. Toss with dressing.

CRANBERRY FLAMBE on ICE CREAM

½ cup honey
¼ cup water
1 Tbs. Curacao
½ tsp. finely shredded orange peel
½ tsp. finely shredded lemon peel

1 pkg. (12 oz.) fresh cranberries,
   washed and sorted
⅛ cup brandy
Vanilla ice cream

Combine honey, water, Curacao and peels in chafing dish or frying pan. Bring to a boil, add cranberries, simmer gently uncovered, for 5 minutes, stirring constantly, until skins pop and sauce is slightly thickened. Warm brandy over low heat. Ignite and pour over berries. Stir until blaze dies out. Serve on ice cream. Serves 6.

Note: Freeze cranberries in the plastic bag in which they are purchased. Use all year long.

Sausage Clam Loaf

Baked Potatoes

Zucchini Saute

Marinated Tomatoes

Sherbet

SAUSAGE CLAM LOAF

1 lb. pork sausage
1 egg
1 cup crushed saltines

1 small onion, minced
1 can (6½ oz.) clams and liquid
⅛ tsp. salt

Mix ingredients together and place in greased loaf pan. Bake 1 hour at 350°. Pour off grease. Let stand 5 minutes before serving. Serves 4.

Note: This is also good served cold as an appetizer.

ZUCCHINI SAUTE

4 zucchini
3 Tbs. butter
1 tsp. dillweed
Salt and pepper

½ cup sour cream
1 Tbs. lemon juice
1 tsp. paprika

Cut squash into ¼-inch slices. Saute in butter, dillweed, salt and pepper for 5 minutes. Mix sour cream, lemon and paprika. Add to zucchini. Heat but do not boil.

Pesto Dip

Shrimp Stuffed Fillet of Sole

Rice Pilaf

Green Beans with Almonds

Fresh Cherry Pie

Oregon Gewurztraminer

PESTO DIP

1 cup finely chopped cooked
   spinach
2 cups cottage cheese
2 Tbs. lemon juice
3 Tbs. milk

½ tsp. Italian seasoning
1 tsp. dried basil or 1 Tbs. fresh
½ cup chopped parsley
1-2 cloves garlic, minced
1 tsp. salt

Mix all ingredients in food processor until smooth. Serve with assorted raw vegetables. Also good on potatoes.

SHRIMP STUFFED FILLET of SOLE

3 Tbs. butter
3 Tbs. flour
1 cup light cream
½ cup milk
1 cup grated Gruyere cheese
½ tsp. salt

⅛ tsp. white pepper
2 Tbs. white wine
1 cup small cooked shrimp,
   chopped
1 Tbs. chopped parsley
6 medium fillets of sole

Melt butter and blend in flour. Stir for 1 minute. Add cream and milk stirring constantly until thickened. Reduce heat; add cheese, salt and pepper and stir until cheese is melted. Blend in wine. Combine shrimp and parsley with 3 Tbs. of cheese sauce. Spoon a strip of mixture lengthwise on each fillet. Roll fillets over stuffing and place seam side down in buttered 12x7½x2 baking dish. Pour remaining sauce over to cover. Bake 30 minutes at 350°. Serve with Rice Pilaf (page 11). Serves 4.

GREEN BEANS with ALMONDS

½ cup sliced almonds
2 Tbs. butter
3 cups cooked fresh green beans

¼ tsp. salt
Pepper

Stir-cook almonds in butter until lightly browned. Add beans, salt and pepper and stir.

FRESH CHERRY PIE

4 cups pitted pie cherries
1¹/₃ cups sugar
4 Tbs. flour

2 drops almond flavoring
2 Tbs. butter
Pastry for 9-inch double crust pie

Combine sugar, flour and almond flavoring with cherries. Arrange in pie pan lined with pastry. Dot with butter. Roll out top crust. Cut ½ inch larger than pie pan. Tuck top crust under bottom crust then crimp edge and prick. Bake 10 minutes at 450°. Reduce heat and bake 30 minutes longer at 350°.

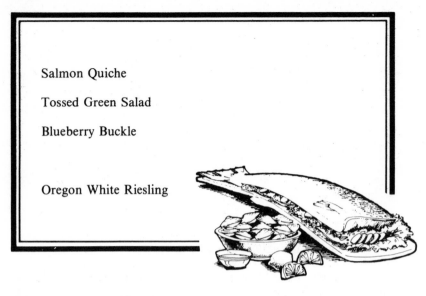

Salmon Quiche

Tossed Green Salad

Blueberry Buckle

Oregon White Riesling

SALMON QUICHE

Crust:

1 cup whole wheat flour
¾ cup sharp Cheddar cheese, grated
¼ cup chopped almonds

½ tsp. salt
¼ tsp. paprika
6 Tbs. corn oil

Combine all ingredients, reserving ½ cup for topping. Press remainder into bottom and sides of a 9-inch pie pan. Bake 10 minutes at 400°. Cool.

Filling:

1 can (15½ oz.) salmon, drain and reserve liquid
3 beaten eggs
1 cup sour cream
¼ cup mayonnaise

½ cup shredded Cheddar cheese
1 Tbs. grated onion
¼ tsp. dill weed
3 drops hot pepper sauce

Add water to salmon liquid to make ½ cup. Flake salmon. Combine remaining ingredients and stir in salmon and liquid. Spoon filling into crust. Sprinkle reserved crust mixture on top. Bake 45 minutes at 325°. Serves 6.

BLUEBERRY BUCKLE

³/₄ cup sugar
¹/₄ cup shortening or margarine
1 egg
¹/₂ cup milk
2 cups flour

2 tsp. baking powder
¹/₂ tsp. salt
Dash of nutmeg
1 tsp. vanilla
2¹/₂ cups blueberries, well drained

Mix sugar, shortening and egg together thoroughly. Add milk. Sift dry ingredients together. Add to first mixture. Add vanilla and fold in blueberries. Spread batter in greased, floured 9-inch square pan. Spread on topping and bake 45-50 minutes at 375°.

Topping:
¹/₂ cup sugar
¹/₃ cup flour

¹/₂ tsp. cinnamon
¹/₄ cup soft butter

Mix together with a fork.

Pacific Baked Salmon Supreme

New Potatoes and Parsley

Peas and Mushroom Saute

Melon Ball Salad with Poppyseed Dressing

Chocolate Amaretto Cheesecake

Washington Riesling

PACIFIC BAKED SALMON SUPREME

½ cup sour cream
½ cup seeded and diced cucumber
¼ cup green olives, sliced
½ tsp. chopped lemon peel

1 Tbs. chopped parsley
¼ tsp. salt
¼ tsp. dill weed
3-5 lbs. salmon

Combine first seven ingredients and spread in cavity and on top of salmon. Wrap in heavy foil and bake 12-15 minutes to the pound at 450°. Remove skin and place on warm platter. Serve with Lemon Butter.

Lemon Butter:
Juice of one lemon
¼ cup butter, melted

2 Tbs. chopped parsley

PEAS and MUSHROOM SAUTE

½ lb. mushrooms, sliced
¼ cup butter
1 pkg. (10 oz.) peas

¼ tsp. salt
¼ tsp. fines herbes
⅛ tsp. white pepper

Saute mushrooms in butter. Add peas and cook 5 minutes or until slightly tender. Add seasonings.

MELON BALL SALAD

1½ cups cantaloupe balls
1½ cups watermelon balls

1 cup red raspberries

Combine melon balls and raspberries. Serve with Poppy Seed Dressing.

Poppy Seed Dressing:

2 Tbs. honey
½ tsp. dry mustard
½ tsp. paprika
2½ Tbs. lemon juice

¼ tsp. grated lemon peel
½ cup salad oil
½ Tbs. poppy seeds

Blend honey, mustard, paprika, lemon juice and peel in food processor. Add oil slowly. Stir in poppy seed.

CHOCOLATE AMARETTO CHEESECAKE

Have all ingredients at room temperature.

Crust:

½ lb. butter, melted
3 cups crushed graham crackers

1 Tbs. Amaretto

Mix butter, crackers and Amaretto. Line the bottom and sides of a 10x13 springform pan with the mixture. Pat down with your fingers. Chill.

Filling:

2 lbs. cream cheese
2 cups sugar
4 large eggs
1 pkg. (12 oz.) semi-sweet
    chocolate chips, melted

1 Tbs. cocoa
2 tsp. vanilla
1 tsp. Amaretto
2 cups sour cream

Beat cream cheese with electric beater until fluffy. Beat in sugar. Add eggs one at a time beating thoroughly between each addition. Add chocolate, cocoa, vanilla and Amaretto. Stir in sour cream. Pour into chilled crust. Bake 1 hour at 325°. Cool on a cake rack (will look runny but is not). Chill at least 5 hours or overnight.

Note: Place pan on a cookie sheet to bake as some butter leaks out.

Seafood

Fillet of Sole with Filbert Sauce

Parmesan Rice

Vegetables Au Gratin

Mixed Green Salad

Hood River Baked Apples

FILLET of SOLE with FILBERT SAUCE

¼ cup flour
1 tsp. paprika
1 tsp. salt
¼ tsp. pepper
1½-2 lbs. fillets of sole

¾ cup butter, divided
½ cup chopped filberts
¼ cup lemon juice
¼ cup chopped parsley

Combine flour, paprika, salt and pepper. Coat fillets. Brown fillets in ½ cup butter 10-15 minutes or until flaky. Remove to a warm platter. Add remaining ¼ cup butter to skillet and saute nuts until lightly browned. Stir in lemon juice and parsley. Heat and pour over sole.

VEGETABLES AU GRATIN

*½ lb. fresh cauliflower, cut
   in flowerets
½ lb. fresh broccoli, cut
   in flowerets
Milk
3 Tbs. butter*

*2 Tbs. flour
¾ cup grated Cheddar cheese
½ tsp. salt
Pepper
¼ cup grated Parmesan cheese*

Cook cauliflower and broccoli in ¾ cup water for 5 minutes. Drain, reserving liquid. Add enough milk to water to make 1¼ cups. Place vegetables in baking dish. In a saucepan melt butter and stir in flour. Add vegetable liquid and milk all at once. Stir-cook until thickened. Add Cheddar cheese and cook until cheese melts. Add salt and pepper. Pour sauce over vegetables. Top with Parmesan cheese. Bake 20 minutes at 350°.

MIXED GREEN SALAD

*Endive, romaine, limestone
   lettuce, torn
1 avocado, sliced
2 tomatoes, cut up*

*1 cucumber, sliced
3 green onions, sliced
½ cup garlic croutons*

Mix with Creamy Garlic Dressing (page 91).

HOOD RIVER BAKED APPLES

*6 large baking apples
1 cup sugar
2 Tbs. grated orange peel*

*½ tsp. cinnamon
3 Tbs. butter
1 cup boiling water*

Wash and core apples. Place in baking dish. Combine sugar, grated orange peel and cinnamon. Fill center of each apple with sugar mixture. Dot each apple with butter. Pour boiling water into baking dish. Bake, uncovered, 1 hour at 375°. Baste apples occasionally. Serve warm or cold.

Note: Add any left over sugar mixture to the water in baking dish.

Steamer Clams or Mussels

Mixed Green Salad with House Dressing

Cheese Bread

Carrot Walnut Cake

Oregon Chardonnay

STEAMER CLAMS or MUSSELS

*3-4 dozen fresh steamer clams in
    the shell, or fresh mussels
1 cup chicken broth
1 cup white wine*

*1 clove garlic, split
½ bay leaf
2 sprigs parsley
Dash of pepper*

Wash and scrub clams. Bring broth, wine, garlic, bay leaf, parsley and pepper to a boil. Add clams; cover and steam 5-10 minutes until shells open. Place clams in individual bowls. Pour nectar over (about ¼ cup). Serve with melted butter in small bowls for dipping.

Note: The season for coastal mussels is from November through April. Pick mussels from ledges or rocks at low tide in unrestricted area. Mussels do not keep. Refrigerate immediately and use the same day as harvested. To clean: Remove beards with a knife. Discard any that are not firmly closed. Soak in fresh water one hour. Drain and scrub.

HOUSE DRESSING

1 cup salad oil
¼ cup sugar
1 tsp. salt
Dash of pepper and paprika

2 tsp. onion powder
2 Tbs. lemon juice
1 cup catsup
½ cup cider vinegar

Place in a jar and shake thoroughly.

CHEESE BREAD

½ cup butter, softened
2 cups grated sharp Cheddar cheese

¼ cup grated Parmesan cheese
1 loaf French bread, cut lengthwise

Mix butter and cheeses. Spread on cut side of bread. Broil until bubbly.

CARROT-WALNUT CAKE

2 cups sugar
4 eggs
1¹/₃ cups vegetable oil
2 cups sifted flour
2 tsp. baking soda

2 tsp. baking powder
2 tsp. cinnamon
4 cups grated carrots
¾ cup coarsely chopped walnuts

Beat sugar and eggs until well mixed. Add other ingredients and fold in carrots and nuts. Pour into greased 9x13 glass baking dish and bake 45-50 minutes at 350°. Ice with Cream Cheese Frosting (page 87) when cool.

Broiled Salmon Steaks with Cucumber Sauce

Parmesan Oven Rice

Broccoli Tomato Cups

Spinach Mushroom Salad

Frosty Strawberry Squares

Oregon or Washington
White Riesling

BROILED SALMON STEAKS

¼ cup oil
3 Tbs. lemon juice
¼ cup chopped parsley
¼ tsp. salt

Freshly grated pepper
4 salmon steaks
Lemon wedges

Combine oil, juice, parsley, salt and pepper. Pour over steaks and marinate 2 hours at room temperature. Drain, reserving marinade. Place on broiler and broil 8-10 minutes. Baste and turn carefully. Baste again and broil 8 minutes longer. Serve with Cucumber Sauce and lemon wedges.

Cucumber Sauce:

1 medium cucumber, peeled lengthwise, seeded and finely chopped
2 Tbs. green pepper, finely chopped (optional)
2 Tbs. green onion, chopped
¼ tsp. tarragon

1 Tbs. lemon juice
¼ tsp. salt
1 tsp. sugar
1 Tbs. chopped parsley
1 cup sour cream
½ tsp. dillweed

Combine all ingredients. Chill at least 1 hour.

PARMESAN RICE

3 Tbs. butter or margarine
2/3 cup rice
1½ cups chicken broth
¼ cup grated Parmesan cheese

2 Tbs. chopped parsley
½ tsp. salt
Dash pepper

In medium skillet melt butter; add rice. Cook and stir until rice is coated and light golden brown. Add remaining ingredients. Cover and cook 20-30 minutes. Fluff with a fork.

BROCCOLI TOMATO CUPS

1 bunch broccoli, separated into
  flowerets
3 tomatoes, cut in half and pulp
  scooped out leaving outer edge
  of tomato intact. Turn upside
  down to drain.

¼ cup butter
1 clove garlic, minced
¼ tsp. salt
Parmesan cheese

Cook broccoli until tender crisp, about 6-8 minutes. Rinse under cold water and dry. Chop into small pieces. Saute broccoli and garlic in butter about 1-2 minutes. Add salt and pepper. Fill tomato cups. Place in buttered baking dish. Sprinkle with Parmesan cheese. Bake 15-20 minutes at 325°.

SPINACH MUSHROOM SALAD

1 lb. spinach, washed, dried and
  torn into bite-size pieces
1 cup Swiss cheese, coarsely
  grated

6-8 mushrooms, sliced
¼ lb. bacon, cooked and
  crumbled
3 eggs, hard-cooked and chopped

Place spinach in large bowl. Add cheese, mushrooms, bacon and eggs. Toss with dressing.

Dressing:
2 Tbs. white wine vinegar
1 tsp. sherry
1 egg yolk
1 tsp. Dijon mustard

¼ tsp. tarragon
¼ tsp. salt
Freshly ground pepper
1 cup oil

Combine all ingredients except oil. Blend with a whisk. Slowly add oil in a steady stream whisking constantly.

FROSTY STRAWBERRY SQUARES

½ cup melted butter	*⅔ cup granulated sugar*
¼ cup brown sugar	*2 cups fresh strawberries, crushed*
1 cup sifted flour	*½ cup sugar*
½ cup walnuts, chopped	*2 Tbs. lemon juice*
2 egg whites	*½ pint whipping cream, whipped*

Stir together the first 4 ingredients. Spread evenly in a shallow pan. Bake at 350° for 20 minutes. Stir occasionally to make crumbs. Sprinkle ⅔ of crumbs in a 13x9x2 pan. Combine egg whites and ⅔ cup sugar. Beat with rotary beater to form stiff peaks, about 10 minutes. Mix strawberries with ½ cup sugar and lemon juice and add to egg whites. Fold in whipped cream. Spoon over crumb mixture. Top with remaining crumbs. Freeze 6 hours or overnight.

Better Than Restaurant Sole

Rice-Vegetable Stack

Dilled Cucumbers

Old Fashioned Strawberry Shortcake

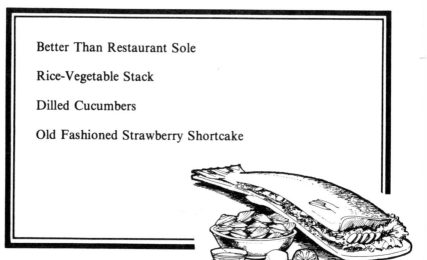

BETTER THAN RESTAURANT SOLE

2 lbs. fillet of sole
Lemon salt or seasoning salt or
*   dillweed*
½-1 cup sour cream

Parmesan cheese
Paprika
Chopped parsley and chives

Place fish in buttered baking dish. Sprinkle on seasonings. Cover with sour cream. Sprinkle with Parmesan cheese, paprika, parsley and chives. Bake at 400° for 10-15 minutes depending on thickness of fish.

Variation:
Add ½ cup chopped green onions.

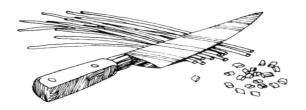

RICE-VEGETABLE STACK

½ small onion, chopped
1-2 celery ribs, sliced
4 mushrooms, sliced
3 Tbs. margarine
1 can (14 oz.) regular strength
  chicken broth

1 pkg. (5 oz.) long grain and
  wild rice
1 zucchini, shredded
1 Tbs. lemon juice
8-9 tomato slices, ½" thick

Saute onion, celery and mushrooms in margarine until tender. Add broth, rice and seasoning packet. Bring to a boil, cover and reduce heat to low. Cook 25 minutes until moisture is absorbed. Cook zucchini in a small amount of boiling water for 1 minute. Drain and blot with paper towel. Add lemon juice and combine with rice. Place tomato slices on greased baking dish. Mound the rice mixture on top of each slice. Bake 10 minutes at 375°.

DILLED CUCUMBERS

1 Tbs. sugar
¼ tsp. salt
⅛ tsp. white pepper
½ cup white vinegar

1 Tbs. fresh chopped dill or ½ tsp.
  dried dillweed
2-3 cucumbers, thinly sliced

Mix sugar, salt, pepper, vinegar and dill. Pour over cucumbers. Chill several hours.

OLD FASHIONED STRAWBERRY SHORTCAKE

Topping:
1 qt. strawberries, hulled and cut
  in half
½ cup sugar

1 cup whipping cream
2 Tbs. confectioners' sugar

Mix strawberries and sugar and refrigerate. Whip cream and add confectioners' sugar.

Shortcake:

2 cups all-purpose flour
3 tsp. baking powder
½ tsp. salt

3 Tbs. sugar
⅓ cup butter, cut into pieces
¾ cup half and half

Combine dry ingredients and add butter. With pastry blender or 2 knives held sideways cut butter into flour until the mixture forms small crumbs. Using a fork stir in half and half until blended. Form dough and knead 8-10 times. Roll out on floured board to ½ inch thick. Cut rounds with a 3-inch cutter. Place on ungreased baking sheet and bake 10-12 minutes at 450°. Cool on a rack.

To assemble: Slit each biscuit in two. Add berries and cream to bottom half. Top with other half and add more berries and whipped cream.

Seafood

Party Cheese Ball

Salmon Florentine

New Potatoes with Parmesan Cheese

Creamy Cucumber Mold

Sourdough Bread

Fruit Cobbler

Oregon Chardonnay

PARTY CHEESE BALL

*2 pkgs. (8 oz. each) cream cheese,
  room temperature*
3 Tbs. horseradish
1 cup grated Parmesan cheese

*1 can (5½ oz.) green stuffed
  olives, drained and chopped,
  reserve liquid*

Blend cream cheese, horseradish, Parmesan cheese, olives and 1 Tbs. olive liquid. Shape into a ball. Chill. Serve with crackers.

SALMON FLORENTINE

4-6 salmon steaks
Butter
Salt
½ cup white wine
Onion slices
½ lemon, sliced

2 bunches spinach
1 clove garlic
½ tsp. tarragon
¼ tsp. salt
⅛ tsp. pepper
2 Tbs. butter

Place salmon in a heavily buttered baking dish. Sprinkle with salt. Pour wine over. Top with onion and lemon slices. Cover lightly and bake 10 minutes at 350°. Cook spinach 2-3 minutes tossing several times. Season with garlic, tarragon, salt, pepper and butter. Place on heated platter. Remove salmon with slotted spatula and lay on top of spinach. Serve with Hollandaise Sauce (page 11).

NEW POTATOES with PARMESAN CHEESE

5-6 new potatoes, scrubbed and
   not peeled
Butter

Salt and pepper
Parsley
Parmesan cheese

Cut each potato into ½ inch slices. Steam until tender (about 15 minutes). Mix with butter, salt, pepper and parsley. Toss lightly. Arrange on a platter with slices overlapping. Sprinkle with Parmesan cheese.

CREAMY CUCUMBER MOLD

1 cup beef broth
1 envelope unflavored gelatin
3 Tbs. sugar
1 cup sour cream
½ tsp. dry mustard

½ tsp. dill weed
2½ Tbs. tarragon vinegar
2 medium cucumbers, seeded,
   shredded and drained
1 Tbs. chopped green onions

Heat beef broth. Add gelatin and sugar and stir to dissolve. Mix sour cream, mustard, dill weed and vinegar. Add cucumbers, onions and gelatin mixture. Pour into 1-quart mold and chill until firm.

FRUIT COBBLER

3-4 cups fruit (peaches, berries,
   rhubarb, etc.) Choose one
Sugar
Salt

Spread fruit on bottom of baking dish. Add enough sugar to sweeten and a dash of salt. Cover with Sour Cream Topping and bake 40 minutes at 350°.

Sour Cream Topping:

1 cup flour
¾ cup sugar
1 tsp. baking powder

½ tsp. salt
1 egg, beaten
½ cup sour cream

Mix dry ingredients together. Add egg and sour cream. Spread over fruit.

Butter Fried Halibut with Vegetable Garnish

Buffet Potatoes

Summer Spinach Salad

Strawberry or Raspberry Mousse

Washington Chardonnay

BUTTER FRIED HALIBUT

*2 lbs. halibut, cut in serving-size
  pieces
2-3 Tbs. butter (not margarine)
Lemon*

*Chopped parsley
Salt and pepper*

Fry halibut in butter about 5 minutes on each side. Add a squeeze of lemon on each piece. Season with salt and pepper. Sprinkle with parsley. Serve with Vegetable Garnish.

Vegetable Garnish:
*2 carrots, grated
4 green onions, chopped
8 mushrooms, sliced*

*3 Tbs. butter
1 tomato, chopped
2 Tbs. chopped parsley*

Saute carrots, green onions and mushrooms several minutes in butter. Add tomato and parsley and cook slightly. Place on top of halibut or to the side.

BUFFET POTATOES

6 large new potatoes
1 cup sharp cheese, grated
4-6 green onions, chopped
1 pint sour cream

$\frac{1}{2}$ tsp. salt
$\frac{1}{8}$ tsp. pepper
2 Tbs. poppy seed

Boil potatoes 15 minutes. Peel (if desired) and grate. Mix with remaining ingredients. Place in a greased casserole. Bake 45 minutes at 325°. Serves 5-6.

SUMMER SPINACH SALAD

1 large bunch spinach, torn
3 eggs, hard-cooked and chopped
5-6 strips bacon, cooked and
    chopped

4 green onions, sliced
1 cup jack cheese, cubed

Dressing:

$\frac{2}{3}$ cup vegetable oil
$\frac{1}{3}$ cup catsup
$\frac{1}{4}$ cup red wine vinegar
$\frac{1}{4}$ cup chopped onion

1 tsp. Worcestershire sauce
$\frac{1}{4}$ cup sugar
$\frac{1}{4}$ tsp. salt
Freshly ground pepper

Mix in a jar and shake well. Use only enough to moisten salad.

Variation:

Use Cheddar cheese in place of
    Jack.

Add sliced mushrooms.
Garnish with tomato wedges.

STRAWBERRY or RASPBERRY MOUSSE

2 cups whipping cream, whipped
$\frac{1}{2}$ cup confectioners' sugar
$\frac{1}{4}$ tsp. salt

1 tsp. gelatin
1 Tbs. fruit juice
1 cup pureed fruit

Add sugar and salt to whipped cream. Soften gelatin in fruit juice. Dissolve over a pan of hot water. Stir into fruit. Fold in whipped cream mixture. Cover and freeze until firm.

Creamy Dill Dip

Northwest Cioppino

Tossed Salad

French Bread

Apple Pie

Oregon Pinot Noir

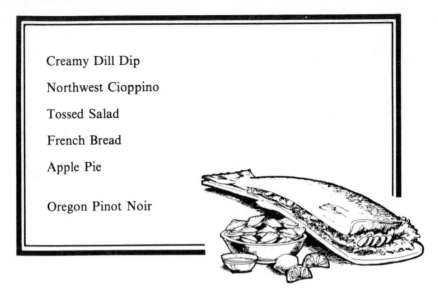

CREAMY DILL DIP

*8 oz. cream cheese at room
    temperature*
¼ cup mayonnaise
⅛ tsp. salt

½ tsp. dried dillweed
2 Tbs. chopped green onions
2 Tbs. chopped parsley
1-1½ Tbs. cream or milk

Blend with electric mixer. Serve with raw vegetables.

NORTHWEST CIOPPINO

1 onion, chopped
2 cloves garlic, minced
1 small green pepper, chopped
2-3 Tbs. oil
1 can (28 oz.) whole tomatoes
1 can (8 oz.) tomato sauce
1 cup white wine
2-3 lemon slices
1½ tsp. salt
½ tsp. pepper

½ tsp. thyme
¼ tsp. oregano
¼ tsp. basil
½ lb. shrimp, shelled and deveined
*1½ lbs. white fish (halibut,
    red snapper, ling cod, or
    scallops, or a combination)*
*1½ dozen steamer clams,
    scrubbed and rinsed*
¼ cup chopped parsley

Saute onion, garlic and green pepper in oil until soft. Add tomatoes and
tomato sauce, wine, lemon slices and seasonings. Simmer 20 minutes.
Add fish and shrimp and simmer 10 minutes. Add clams. Cover and
cook until clams open. Discard any clams that do not open. Add
parsley.

APPLE PIE

6-7 cups apples, peeled and sliced
3/4-1 cup sugar
2-3 Tbs. flour
1/4 tsp. cinnamon

1/8 tsp. nutmeg
1 tsp. lemon juice
1 1/2 Tbs. butter
Pastry for double-crust pie

Mix apples with sugar, flour, cinnamon, nutmeg and lemon juice. Place in unbaked pie shell. Dot with butter. Cover with top crust. Sprinkle with sugar and prick for air holes. Bake 10 minutes at 450°. Reduce heat and bake 35-45 minutes longer.

Baybridge Barbecued Crab

Vegetable Slaw

French Bread

Fresh Pear Cake

Oregon White Riesling

BAYBRIDGE BARBECUED CRAB

1 can (46 oz.) tomato juice
2 cans (28 oz.) whole tomatoes
3 Tbs. sugar
½ cup vinegar
½ cup catsup
1 Tbs. prepared mustard
4 Tbs. Worcestershire sauce
2 bay leaves
3 sprigs parsley
4 celery ribs with a few leaves,
*   cut up*

1 onion, chopped
2 cloves garlic, cut up
1 tsp. chili powder
1 lemon, sliced
2 tsp. salt
1 tsp. pepper
6 crabs, cooked, cleaned and cut
*   in half*

Combine all ingredients except crab and simmer 1 hour. Remove bay leaves and lemon slices. Puree in food processor. Scrub crab thoroughly and heat in sauce about 10 minutes. Place crab on each plate with a bowl of sauce for dipping. Serves 8-10.

VEGETABLE SLAW

(page 109).

FRESH PEAR CAKE

1½ cups oil	*1 tsp. baking powder*
2 cups sugar	*1 tsp. cinnamon*
3 eggs, beaten	*1 tsp. vanilla*
3 cups flour	*2 cups chopped ripe but firm pears*
1 tsp. salt	*1 cup chopped nuts*

Mix oil, sugar and eggs together. Sift dry ingredients together. Add to oil mixture. Add vanilla, pears and nuts. Bake in a greased 10" Bundt pan for 1 hour 20 minutes at 325°. Cool in pan ½ hour. Dust with confectioners' sugar.

Cracked Crab with Sauces

Overnight Layered Salad

Garlic Bread

Blueberries and Cream

Northwest Beer

CRACKED CRAB with SAUCES

Arrange well chilled, cooked, cleaned, cracked crab on individual plates. Allow about 1 pound for each serving. Serve with sauces of your choice.

Lemon Mustard Sauce:

1 cup mayonnaise
1 Tbs. lemon juice

1 tsp. grated lemon peel
1 tsp. Dijon-style mustard

Combine all ingredients. Cover and refrigerate.

Cocktail Sauce:

2 cups catsup
1½-2 Tbs. horseradish
2 Tbs. lemon juice

½ tsp. salt
1 tsp. Worcestershire sauce
2-3 drops hot pepper sauce

Combine and mix well.

Hot Piquant Sauce:

½ cup chili sauce
¼ cup lemon juice
¼ cup butter

2 tsp. Worcestershire sauce
1 tsp. sugar

Mix well and heat. Serve hot.

Tartar Sauce:

1 cup mayonnaise
1 dill pickle, chopped
2 Tbs. chopped green onion
1 Tbs. mashed capers

1 tsp. white wine vinegar or
  lemon juice
Dash of cayenne

Mix well and chill.

Aioli Sauce (Garlic Sauce):

4 cloves garlic, peeled
1 egg yolk
1/2 tsp. salt

Dash white pepper
1/2 cup olive oil
1/2 cup other light vegetable oil

Put garlic cloves through a garlic press. Put the resulting puree in a blender with the egg yolk, salt and pepper. Blend at lowest speed for a few moments. While continuing to blend, add oils slowly, drop-by-drop at first, faster when mixture begins to thicken. This is a thick sauce similar to mayonnaise.

OVERNIGHT LAYERED SALAD

1 medium head iceberg lettuce,
  shredded
1/2 cup sliced green onions
1 cup sliced mushrooms

1 cup sliced celery
1 can (8 oz.) water chestnuts,
  drained and sliced
1 pkg. (10 oz.) frozen peas

Layer all ingredients in a long dish or large bowl. Spread evenly with Mayonnaise Dressing. Cover and refrigerate overnight.

Mayonnaise Dressing:

2 cups mayonnaise
2 tsp. sugar
1/2 cup grated Parmesan cheese

1 tsp. seasoned salt
1/4 tsp. garlic powder

Mix well. Add topping before serving.

Topping:

1/2 lb. bacon, cubed and cooked
3 hard-cooked eggs, chopped

Perch Mozzarella, Del

Brown Rice

Carrot and Zucchini Julienne

Fruit Platter

Walnut Brownies

Oregon Merlot

PERCH MOZZARELLA, DEL

6 perch fillets (4 oz. each)
½ cup flour
2 eggs
1 tsp. salt
⅛ tsp. white pepper
¾ cup fine dry bread crumbs

⅓ cup grated Parmesan cheese
½ cup butter
2 cans (8 oz. each) tomato sauce
½ tsp. basil
½ tsp. oregano
6 slices Mozzarella cheese

Coat fillets with flour. Dip first into a mixture of the eggs, salt and pepper, then into a mixture of bread crumbs and Parmesan. Heat butter in skillet, add fillets and brown on both sides over medium heat. Arrange browned fillets in a 2-quart baking dish. Mix tomato sauce, basil and oregano; pour over fish. Top each fillet with a slice of cheese. Bake 15 minutes at 350°. Serve with Brown Rice (page 121).

CARROT and ZUCCHINI JULIENNE

3 medium carrots, peeled
2 medium zucchini, scrubbed
2 Tbs. butter

2 Tbs. chopped fresh dill
Salt and white pepper to taste

Cut carrots and zucchini into strips about 3 inches long and ¼ inch wide. Place carrots in a steamer over boiling water and cover. Steam for 6 minutes. Add zucchini and steam 8-10 minutes longer. Transfer vegetables to a large bowl. Melt butter in a small saucepan; sprinkle with dill. Pour over steamed vegetables and toss to combine. Season to taste.

FRESH FRUIT PLATTER

1 ripe cantaloupe, peeled and
*   sliced*
2 oranges, sliced
2 ripe avocados, sliced

2 ripe pears, sliced
¼ cup lemon juice
Seedless green grapes
Strawberries, washed and hulled

Pour lemon juice on avocados and pears. Arrange fruit on a platter. Serve with dressing.

Dressing:
½ cup whipping cream, whipped
½ cup mayonnaise

1 Tbs. honey

Fold mayonnaise and honey into whipped cream.

WALNUT BROWNIES

4 oz. unsweetened chocolate
1 cup butter
4 eggs
2 cups sugar
1 tsp. vanilla

1 cup flour
½ tsp. baking powder
¼ tsp. salt
2 cups walnuts, coarsely chopped

Melt chocolate and butter in double boiler or over low heat. Cool slightly. Beat eggs until fluffy. Add sugar, vanilla and chocolate mixture. Sift flour, baking powder and salt together. Add to chocolate mixture. Dust walnuts with some flour and add. Pour into a 9x13-inch buttered baking dish. Bake 30 minutes at 325°. Spread with frosting when cool.

Frosting:

¼ cup butter or margarine
1 square unsweetened chocolate
3 Tbs. milk

½ lb. confectioners' sugar
½ tsp. vanilla

Heat butter, chocolate and milk in a saucepan, stirring constantly until chocolate is melted. Beat with sugar and vanilla until smooth.

Sauteed Almond Oysters

Fettucini

Green Salad

Fruit and Nut Basket

Washington Sauvignon Blanc

SAUTEED ALMOND OYSTERS

1 egg	*3 Tbs. chopped almonds*
2 Tbs. milk	*1-2 Tbs. chopped parsley*
½ tsp. salt	*2 doz. oysters, rinsed and drained*
¼ tsp. oregano	*¼-⅓ cup butter*
⅔ cup crushed saltines	*Lemon wedges*

Mix egg with milk, salt and oregano. Combine saltines, almonds and parsley. Dip oysters in egg mixture and then in cracker mixture. Saute lightly in butter 5-6 minutes until firm. Serve with lemon wedges. Serves 4.

FETTUCINI

6 oz. fettucini noodles	*¼ tsp. salt*
¼ cup butter	*Freshly ground pepper*
½ cup light cream	*1 Tbs. chopped parsley*
¼ cup freshly grated Parmesan cheese	

Cook noodles in large pan of boiling salted water. Drain in colander. Melt butter in pan. Add cream and bring to boil. Reduce heat. Add cheese and stir until melted. Return noodles to pan and toss. Add salt, pepper and parsley and mix gently.

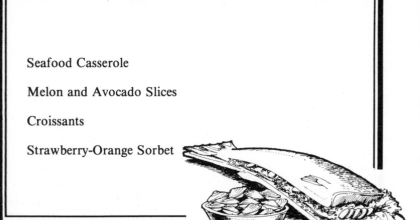

Seafood Casserole

Melon and Avocado Slices

Croissants

Strawberry-Orange Sorbet

SEAFOOD CASSEROLE

2 cups mayonnaise
*¼ cup green onions with some
   tops, chopped*
¼ cup minced parsley
*2 cups bread cubes, crusts
   removed*
4 eggs, hard-cooked and chopped
¾ lb. crab
¾ lb. small cooked shrimp

*1 can (14 oz.) water packed
   artichoke hearts, drained and
   cut in half*
*1 cup Swiss or Parmesan cheese,
   grated*
¼ cup slivered almonds

Combine first 7 ingredients and mix lightly. Line a buttered baking dish
with artichoke hearts. Add seafood. Pour sauce over. Sprinkle with
cheese and nuts. Bake 40 minutes at 350°. Let stand 5 minutes. Serves 8.
Can be made ahead and refrigerated. Bring to room temperature before
baking.

Sauce:

2 Tbs. butter
½ lb. mushrooms, sliced
1 Tbs. flour
¼ tsp. salt

⅛ tsp. white pepper
1 cup light cream or milk
¼ cup sherry

Saute mushrooms in melted butter until slightly cooked. Add flour and blend. Add salt, pepper, milk and sherry. Stir-cook until thickened. Set aside to cool.

STRAWBERRY-ORANGE SORBET

1¾ cups orange juice
½ cup lemon juice
3 pints strawberries

1¾ cups sugar
⅛ tsp. salt

Blend all ingredients at high speed. Pour into 9x13 pan and cover with plastic wrap. Freeze partially about 1 inch from sides of pan. Put in blender again and mix until well blended. Pour back into the pan and refreeze. May be kept in freezer several weeks.

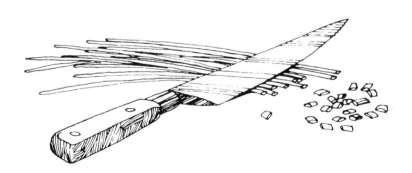

Oyster and Scallop Kabobs

Rice Salad with Lemon-Dill Dressing

French Bread

Strawberry Rhubarb Pie

Washington Sauvignon Blanc

OYSTER and SCALLOP KABOBS

For 4 skewers

8 bacon strips
12 med. scallops, washed and
   drained
12 oysters, rinsed

8 cherry tomatoes
8 mushroom caps
1 green pepper, cut in 1-inch
   squares

Pre-fry bacon slightly. (Bacon should still be limp.) Marinate scallops and oysters 30 minutes.

Marinade:
4 Tbs. lemon juice
¼ cup butter, melted
¼ tsp. salt

⅛ tsp. pepper
½ tsp. dill weed

On a skewer, alternate oysters, green pepper, scallops, tomatoes, ending with a mushroom. Bacon strips are woven between other ingredients. Broil on foil 5 minutes on each side. Baste with marinade.

RICE SALAD with LEMON-DILL DRESSING

3 cups hot cooked rice
½ lb. fresh mushrooms, sliced
3 medium tomatoes, cut in wedges
   and drained

6 slices bacon, cooked and
   crumbled
4 green onions, sliced
Spinach leaves

Mix rice with half of Lemon-Dill Dressing. Stir in mushrooms and tomatoes. Cover and chill. Add bacon and onions and half of remaining dressing. Arrange spinach leaves on a serving plate. Place rice salad on top. Pass remaining dressing.

Lemon-Dill Dressing:

1 cup vegetable oil
⅔ cup lemon juice
1 Tbs. Dijon-style mustard
2 tsp. dill weed
2 cloves garlic, minced

½ tsp. salt
½ tsp. tarragon, crushed
¼ tsp. paprika
¼ tsp. pepper

Combine all ingredients and chill.

FRENCH BREAD with MAYONNAISE TOPPING

1 loaf French bread, split
   lengthwise
1 cup mayonnaise

3 Tbs. Parmesan cheese
¼ tsp. paprika

Mix mayonnaise, Parmesan and paprika. Spread on cut side of bread. Bake 7-8 minutes at 375° until golden. Serves 8.

STRAWBERRY-RHUBARB PIE

1½ lbs. fresh rhubarb, cut into
   ½-inch slices
1 pint fresh strawberries, cut in
   half
1¼ cups sugar
⅓ cup orange juice
2 Tbs. tapioca
2 tsp. grated orange peel
¼ tsp. salt
2 Tbs. butter
2 Tbs. sugar
Pastry for 2-crust pie

Combine rhubarb, berries, 1¼ cups sugar, orange juice, tapioca, orange peel and salt in large bowl. Let stand 15 minutes. Roll out ⅔ of the pastry and place in 9-inch pie plate. Spoon rhubarb mixture into shell. Dot with butter. Roll out remaining pastry into 11x4-inch rectangle; cut lengthwise into ¼-inch strips. Arrange strips in lattice pattern over filling. Trim pastry; seal and flute edge. Sprinkle 2 Tbs. sugar over lattice top. Bake 10 minutes at 425°. Reduce heat to 375° and bake about 1 hour.

Mushroom Appetizer

Oysters Gourmet

Spinach-Rice Casserole

Wilted Leaf Lettuce Salad

Sourdough Bread

Fresh Blueberry Pie

Washington Sauvignon Blanc

MUSHROOM APPETIZER

1 lb. fresh mushroom caps
2 Tbs. butter
½ tsp. seasoning salt
¼ tsp. garlic salt

2 Tbs. dry white wine
½ cup sour cream
Paprika

Clean mushrooms, slice off stems (save for soups). Saute caps in butter. Sprinkle with salts. Add wine. Simmer until tender. Add sour cream and warm. Sprinkle with paprika. Serve with toothpicks.

Seafood

OYSTERS GOURMET

1 jar (16 oz.) small oysters

Wash oysters in a strainer. Arrange in baking dish.

Sprinkle on top:

3/4 tsp. oregano
1 tsp. basil, crushed
1/2 tsp. salt
1 tsp. minced garlic
1/4 tsp. pepper

2 Tbs. lemon juice
1 Tbs. chopped parsley
3/4 cube margarine, melted
Bread crumbs or crushed saltines

Cover lightly with crumbs and bake about 10 minutes at 450°. Serve with French bread for dipping in sauce. Serves 4 as a main course; 6-8 as an appetizer.

Note: If small oysters are not available, cut oysters in half.

SPINACH-RICE CASSEROLE

2 pkgs. (10 oz. each) frozen
  chopped spinach
4 eggs
2/3 cup milk
1/4 cup butter or margarine, melted
1/2 cup onion, finely chopped
2 Tbs. chopped parsley

1 tsp. thyme
1 1/2 tsp. salt
1/4 tsp. nutmeg
1 tsp. Worcestershire sauce
3 cups cooked rice
2 cups sharp Cheddar cheese,
  grated

Cook spinach and drain well. Beat eggs; add remaining ingredients except rice and cheese and mix well. Stir in rice, spinach and cheese. Pour into a 2-quart, buttered casserole and bake uncovered 45 minutes at 350°. Additional cheese may be placed on top for the last 5 minutes of cooking. Serves 6-8.

WILTED LEAF LETTUCE SALAD

*Leaf lettuce, torn in bite-size
    pieces
2 eggs, hard-cooked and chopped
3 green onions, sliced
6 slices bacon, diced
¼ cup bacon drippings
2 Tbs. red wine vinegar*

*2 Tbs. lemon juice
2 tsp. sugar
¼ tsp. salt
¼ tsp. pepper
¼ tsp. dry mustard
½ tsp. Worcestershire sauce*

Place lettuce, eggs and onions in large bowl. Cook bacon and set aside.
Pour off all grease except ¼ cup. Add vinegar, lemon juice, sugar, salt,
pepper, Worcestershire and mustard. Heat and blend. Add bacon to
lettuce. Pour dressing over and toss.

FRESH BLUEBERRY PIE

*9-inch baked pie shell, cooled
4 cups fresh blueberries, washed
    and drained
1 cup sugar
3 Tbs. cornstarch*

*¼ cup water
¼ tsp. salt
1 Tbs. lemon juice
1 Tbs. butter*

Line cooled pie shell with 2 cups berries. Stir-cook remaining berries
with sugar, cornstarch, water and salt over medium heat until thickened. Add lemon juice and butter. Cool. Pour over berries in the shell.
Chill. Serve with ice cream.

Bacon-Cheese Squares

Bay Scallops and Mushrooms in Cream Sauce

Fluffy Rice

Broiled Tomato Halves

Mixed Green Salad

Champagne Compote

Oregon White Riesling

BACON-CHEESE SQUARES

*6-8 slices sandwich bread, crusts
    removed and cut in fourths
6 slices bacon, cooked and
    crumbled
1½ cups grated sharp Cheddar
    cheese*

*½ cup chopped green onions
3 Tbs. mayonnaise
1 tsp. Worcestershire sauce
⅛ tsp. dry mustard*

Toast bread on one side. Combine bacon, cheese and onions. Mix mayonnaise with Worcestershire and mustard and add to cheese mixture. Spread on untoasted side of bread. Broil until bubbly. Serves 4.

BAY SCALLOPS and MUSHROOMS in CREAM SAUCE

1 lb. scallops, rinsed, drained and
   dried
2½ Tbs. butter
½ lb. mushrooms, quartered
3 green onions, sliced
1 clove garlic, minced
½ cup white wine

½ cup half and half
¾ Tbs. Dijon mustard
1 tsp. lemon juice
¼ tsp. salt
Freshly ground pepper
¼ cup chopped parsley

Saute scallops in butter 3 minutes stirring constantly. Place in a serving dish and keep warm. Add mushrooms, onions and garlic and cook 30 seconds. Add wine and boil until reduced to about 2 tablespoons. Add cream and stir until thickened. Stir in mustard, lemon juice, salt and pepper. Return scallops to pan and reheat. Add parsley. Serves 4.

BROILED TOMATO HALVES

2-3 tomatoes, cut in half
Oil
Salt and pepper

Basil
Chopped parsley
Parmesan cheese

Place tomatoes in baking dish. Rub cut side with oil. Sprinkle with remaining ingredients. Broil 6-8 minutes.

CHAMPAGNE COMPOTE

2 fresh pears, peeled and
   quartered
2 fresh peaches, peeled and
   quartered
1 cup strawberries, hulled
1 cup fresh pineapple chunks
½ cup sugar

1 cup cantaloupe balls
1 cup honeydew balls
1 split (⁴/5 pt.) champagne, chilled
  OR
  1 bottle (10 oz.) gingerale
Mint sprigs

Combine pears, peaches, strawberries and pineapple with sugar. Chill 30 minutes. Before serving add cantaloupe, honeydew and champagne. Serve immediately. Garnish with mint sprigs.

Seafood Sandwiches
Coast Crab Melt
      or
Shrimp on a Muffin
      or
Shrimp Boats
Fresh Fruit
Zucchini Drop Cookies

Northwest Beer

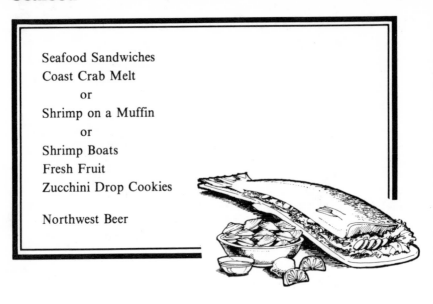

COAST CRAB MELT

½ lb. crab
¼ cup mayonnaise
1 tsp. chili sauce or catsup
¼ tsp. Worcestershire sauce
1 tsp. lemon juice

1 tsp. Dijon mustard
Dash of salt
1 cup grated Cheddar cheese
4 English muffins

Mix crab, mayonnaise, chili sauce, Worcestershire sauce, lemon juice, mustard and salt. Split muffins. Spread with crab mixture. Top with cheese. Broil 3 minutes until bubbly. Serves 4.

SHRIMP on a MUFFIN

3 oz. cream cheese
2 Tbs. mayonnaise
1 Tbs. cocktail sauce
2 drops Tabasco
¼ tsp. dry mustard
Dash of salt

2 hard-cooked eggs, chopped
1 cup small cooked shrimp
2 Tbs. chopped green olives
1 Tbs. chopped green onions
5 English muffins, split

Blend cream cheese, mayonnaise, cocktail sauce, Tabasco, mustard and salt. Add eggs, shrimp, olives and onions. Partially broil muffins. Spread on shrimp mixture. Broil until bubbly. Serves 4-5.

SHRIMP BOATS

1 lb. Cheddar cheese, grated	*15 stuffed olives, sliced*
1 green pepper, chopped	*1 can (8 oz.) tomato sauce*
5 green onions, chopped	*½ cup vegetable oil*
2 cups small cooked shrimp	*1½ dozen hard rolls or buns*

Combine all ingredients except rolls and stir to blend. Cover and refrigerate ½ hour. Open rolls and remove some of the bread to make a small pocket. Fill with shrimp mixture. Wrap several rolls together in foil. Bake at 350° for 15-20 minutes until hot.

ZUCCHINI DROP COOKIES

1 cup sugar	*1 tsp. cinnamon*
½ cup butter	*½ tsp. cloves*
1 egg, beaten	*½ tsp. salt*
1 cup grated zucchini	*¾ cup chopped nuts*
2 cups flour	*¾ cup raisins*
1 tsp. baking soda	

Cream sugar and butter together; add egg and zucchini. Sift together flour, baking soda, cinnamon, cloves and salt and add to zucchini mixture, blending well. Add nuts and raisins and stir in. Drop by spoonsful on greased cookie sheet and bake for 10-12 minutes at 350°.

Seafood

Pan Fried Trout
      or
Barbecued Trout
Baked Potatoes with Topping
Spring Asparagus Salad
French Bread
Blackberry Pie

Washington White Riesling

PAN FRIED TROUT

½ cup cornmeal　　　　*Oil for frying*
½ tsp. salt　　　　　　*6 medium trout*
Pepper

Roll trout in cornmeal, salt and pepper. Fry quickly in enough oil to cover half of trout. Do not crowd and do not let oil smoke. Turn once. Cook about 5-6 minutes on each side. Serve with Herb Butter.

Herb Butter:
¼ cup butter, melted　　*¼ tsp. thyme*
¼ tsp. salt　　　　　　*1 Tbs. chopped chives*
¼ tsp. chervil　　　　　*2 Tbs. chopped parsley*

Combine all ingredients.

BARBECUED TROUT

4-6 medium trout　　　*Salt and pepper*
Lemon juice　　　　　　*Garlic salt*
Melted butter

Season trout well with lemon juice, butter, salt, pepper and garlic salt both inside and out. Wrap in foil and cook on barbecue 3 minutes on one side; turn over and cook another 3-4 minutes. Open foil after turning if a smokey flavor is desired.

BAKED POTATOES with TOPPING

4 potatoes, baked	*¼ tsp. salt*
Butter	*1 green onion, sliced*
1 can (2½ oz.) chopped ripe olives	*Chopped parsley*
1 cup sour cream	

Make a slit in potatoes and squeeze open. Add a pat of butter in each potato. Mix olives, sour cream, salt, onion and parsley. Place a large spoonful on top.

SPRING ASPARAGUS SALAD

2 lbs. fresh asparagus	*¼ tsp. salt*
2 Tbs. sugar	*⅛ tsp. pepper*
½ cup tarragon vinegar	

Cut off tough part of asparagus stalks so all spears are the same length. Cook asparagus until just tender. Plunge into cold water to freshen. Drain and place in a large dish in single layer. Mix sugar, vinegar, salt and pepper and pour over asparagus. Cover and chill 4 hours. Turn once. Drain and reserve 3 Tbs. of marinade. Serve with Topping.

Topping:

⅓ cup sour cream	*3 Tbs. marinade*
⅓ cup mayonnaise	*¼ tsp. dill weed*

BLACKBERRY PIE

1 quart fresh blackberries	*¼ tsp. lemon juice*
1 cup sugar	*2 Tbs. butter*
3 Tbs. tapioca	*Pastry for a 2-crust 9-inch pie*
½ tsp. cinnamon	

Combine berries, sugar, tapioca, cinnamon and lemon juice. Pour into unbaked bottom crust. Dot with butter. Cover with top crust and seal edges. Prick top generously with a fork. Bake 10 minutes at 450°; reduce heat to 350° and bake 35-40 minutes longer.

Poultry

Crab Appetizer

Chicken Breasts and Mushrooms in Lemon Sauce

Fluffy Rice

French-Cut Green Beans

Orange and Green Salad

Filbert Cheesecake

Washington Chardonnay

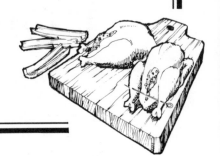

CRAB APPETIZER

1 lb. fresh crab
½ cup mayonnaise

¼ tsp. salt
2 cups grated sharp cheese

Mix crab, mayonnaise and salt. Place in a baking dish. Cover with cheese and bake at 350° until cheese melts. Serve with chips or crackers.

CHICKEN BREASTS and MUSHROOMS in LEMON SAUCE

¼ lb. mushrooms, cut in thick
slices
2 cloves garlic, minced
6 Tbs. butter, divided
4 whole chicken breasts, split,
boned and skinned

⅓ cup flour
½ tsp. salt
¼ tsp. paprika
¼ cup white wine
¼ cup lemon juice
2 Tbs. chopped parsley

Saute mushrooms and garlic in 3 Tbs. butter until lightly browned. Remove with a slotted spoon. Dust chicken with flour and seasonings. Add remaining 3 Tbs. butter to pan and brown chicken on all sides. Set aside. Add wine and lemon juice and bring to a boil. Stir with a wooden spoon to loosen browned bits. Return mushrooms and chicken to the pan. Reduce heat and cook covered 8-10 minutes, until chicken is done. Add parsley. Serves 4-5.

ORANGE and GREEN SALAD

1 head leaf lettuce, torn
1 fresh orange, sliced

1 avocado, sliced
1 sweet white onion, sliced

Dressing:

½ cup oil
2 Tbs. tarragon vinegar
2 Tbs. sugar
½ tsp. salt

1 Tbs. toasted sesame seeds
½ tsp. dry mustard
½ tsp. celery salt
½ Tbs. grated onion

Shake the dressing in a jar and pour over greens, oranges, avocado and onion until greens are coated.

Variation: Add 1 cup small cooked shrimp.

FILBERT CHEESECAKE

Crust:

1½ cups ground vanilla wafers
¾ cup toasted and ground filberts,
    plus 2 Tbs. for topping

2 Tbs. sugar
½ cup melted butter

Filling:

Have all ingredients at room
    temperature
3 pkgs. (8 oz. each) cream cheese

1 cup sugar
3 eggs, beaten
3 Tbs. creme de cacao

Topping:

2 cups sour cream

2 Tbs. sugar

Crust: Combine wafer crumbs, ¾ cup nuts, sugar and butter. Pat mixture into bottom and sides of 8-inch springform pan. Chill 30 minutes. Bake crust 15 minutes at 300°. Cool.

Filling: Beat cream cheese with electric mixer until smooth. Gradually beat in sugar. Add eggs and creme de cacao and blend. Pour into crust. Bake at 350° for 45-50 minutes until set. Let cool slightly.

Topping: Mix sour cream and sugar. Spread over cheesecake to within ½ inch of edge. Bake 5 minutes longer. Sprinkle with 2 Tbs. nuts. Refrigerate 5 hours or overnight. Release edge of pan and remove. Cut in wedges. Serves 12-14.

Dilly Shrimp Dip

Stuffed Chicken Breasts

Rice Pilaf

Broccoli Salad

Strawberry Glace Pie

Oregon Gewurztraminer

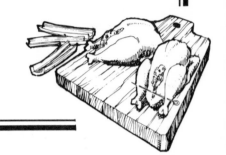

DILLY SHRIMP DIP

1 cup chopped cooked shrimp
1 Tbs. lemon juice
8 oz. cream cheese at room
  temperature
¼ cup milk

¼ cup mayonnaise
2 Tbs. finely chopped green onion
½ tsp. dried dillweed
2-3 drops hot pepper sauce
Dash of salt

Mix shrimp and lemon juice. Beat cream cheese; gradually mix in milk and mayonnaise blending until smooth. Add onion, dillweed, hot pepper sauce and salt. Stir in shrimp. Cover and chill.

STUFFED CHICKEN BREASTS

10 chicken breast pieces (5 whole
    breasts, split, boned and
    skinned)
1 Tbs. lemon juice
Salt
1/4 lb. sweet Italian sausage
    (remove casing)
1/4 cup sliced celery
2 Tbs. chopped onion
5-6 mushrooms, chopped

2 Tbs. butter
1/2 cup soft bread crumbs
2 Tbs. chopped parsley
1/4 tsp. marjoram
1 cup chicken broth
3 Tbs. dry sherry, divided
Salt and pepper
2 Tbs. cornstarch
2 Tbs. water

Pound chicken breasts to 1/4-inch thickness. Brush with lemon juice and salt lightly. Cook sausage, celery, onions and mushrooms in butter until tender. Add bread crumbs, parsley, marjoram and 2 Tbs. sherry. Place a spoonful of mixture on each breast. Roll up and arrange in a greased baking dish seam side down. Mix broth, 1 Tbs. sherry and salt and pepper and pour over. Bake uncovered for 35 minutes at 350°. Baste once. Skim off fat if necessary. Pour sauce into saucepan and add cornstarch mixed with water. Stir-cook until thickened. Pour over chicken. Serves 6-8.

RICE PILAF

2 Tbs. butter
6-8 mushrooms, sliced
1/4 cup chopped onion
1 cup rice

2 cups beef or chicken broth
1/2 tsp. salt
Chopped parsley

Saute mushrooms and onion in butter until partially cooked. Add rice and stir-cook 1 minute. Add remaining ingredients; place in buttered casserole; cover and bake at 350° for 1 hour.

BROCCOLI SALAD

1 bunch fresh broccoli (2 lbs.)
1/4 cup chopped parsley
1/3 cup olive or vegetable oil
1/4 cup white wine vinegar
1 Tbs. prepared mustard

1 clove garlic, minced
1 tsp. salt
1/4 tsp. pepper
2 eggs, hard-cooked and chopped

Trim broccoli and break into flowerets. Slice into 1-inch strips. Mix remaining ingredients except eggs. Combine with broccoli and toss to mix. Chill several hours. To serve, arrange on lettuce leaves and top with eggs.

Note: Broccoli may be steamed 3-4 minutes if desired.

STRAWBERRY GLACE PIE

1 8-inch baked pie shell
2 pints strawberries, washed and
stemmed
½ cup sugar
Dash salt
½ cup water, divided

1½ Tbs. cornstarch
1 Tbs. lemon juice
8 oz. cream cheese, softened
½ cup milk
Whipped cream

Glaze: Slice enough of the berries to make 1 cup. Place sliced berries in saucepan with sugar, salt and ¼ cup of water. Bring to a boil and cook 3 minutes; remove from heat. Mix cornstarch with remaining ¼ cup water and stir into berries. Return to heat and cook, stirring, until thickened, about 2 minutes. Stir in lemon juice. Cool to room temperature.

Beat cream cheese with milk until smooth. Spread in bottom of cooled pie shell. Cover with half the glaze. Arrange reserved whole berries on top, stem ends down. Spoon remaining glaze over berries. Chill for 2 hours. Serve with whipped cream.

King Chicken

Spinach Mushroom Casserole

Fruit Salad with Honey Dressing

French Bread

Fresh Peach Ice Cream

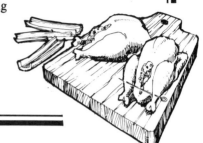

KING CHICKEN

1 large fryer, cut up, plus
* 1 breast, split*
Salt and pepper
1 Tbs. oil
2 Tbs. butter
1 cup sliced mushrooms
1 clove garlic, minced
½ cup chopped onion

1 can (16 oz.) whole tomatoes
⅓ cup white wine
¼ cup tomato paste
1 bay leaf
½ tsp. thyme
¼ tsp. salt
¼ cup chopped parsley

Salt and pepper chicken. Brown in oil and butter. Remove from pan. Add mushrooms, garlic and onion and cook 1 minute. Add tomatoes, wine, tomato paste, bay leaf, thyme and salt. Return chicken to pan. Cover and simmer 40 minutes. Remove lid, add parsley and cook 15 minutes longer. Remove bay leaf before serving. Serves 6.

SPINACH MUSHROOM CASSEROLE

2 pkgs. (10 oz. each) frozen chopped spinach	1/4 tsp. thyme
10 mushrooms, sliced	1/4 tsp. salt
1 Tbs. butter	Freshly ground pepper
1 cup cottage cheese	2 tomatoes, thinly sliced
1/2 tsp. garlic powder	1 cup grated Mozzarella cheese
	2 Tbs. grated Parmesan cheese

Cook spinach. Drain and squeeze dry. Saute mushrooms lightly in butter. Mix spinach, mushrooms, cottage cheese and seasonings. Place in casserole. Lay tomatoes on top. Top with cheeses. Bake 25 minutes at 350°. Serves 6.

FRUIT SALAD with HONEY DRESSING

Red apples, unpeeled and cubed	Walnuts, cut in large pieces
Red grapes, seeded	Bananas
Raisins	Fresh pears (optional)

Honey Dressing:

1/4 cup honey	1/2 tsp. dry mustard
1/2 cup salad oil	1/2 tsp. paprika
1 Tbs. lemon juice	1/4 tsp. salt
2 1/2 Tbs. vinegar	1-2 Tbs. sugar
1/2 tsp. grated onion	

Mix together and use over prepared fruit. Bring to room temperature before using.

FRESH PEACH ICE CREAM

2 lbs. fresh ripe peaches, peeled,
  halved, pits removed
3 Tbs. lemon juice
1½ cups sugar

2 eggs, separated
2 Tbs. confectioners' sugar
1 cup heavy cream, whipped

Place peaches and lemon juice in bowl and crush. Stir in sugar. In another bowl beat egg whites with confectioners' sugar until soft peaks form. Beat egg yolks. Fold yolks into egg whites. Fold in whipped cream. Add crushed peaches. Pour into 1-quart ice cube tray or 8-inch square pan. (Refrigerator should be set on coldest temperature.) Freeze until firm around the edges. Transfer into bowl and beat with rotary beater. Return to tray and freeze until firm and ready to serve.

Swiss Chicken

Noodles or Rice

Steamed Carrots

Club Salad

Hot Rolls

Raspberry Ginger Cream

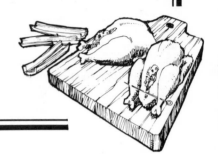

SWISS CHICKEN

4 chicken breasts, split
¼ cup flour
½ tsp. salt
¼ tsp. oregano
¼ tsp. pepper
½ tsp. garlic salt
1 tsp. paprika
2 Tbs. oil

1 Tbs. butter
4 green onions, chopped
10 mushrooms, quartered
½ cup chicken broth
½ cup white wine
½ cup sour cream
1 cup Swiss cheese, grated

Shake chicken in bag containing flour and seasonings. Brown in oil and butter and place in casserole. Stir-cook onions and mushrooms 2 minutes and add to chicken. In the same pan add remaining flour, broth and wine and blend. Pour over chicken. Cover and bake 45 minutes at 350°. Mix sour cream and Swiss cheese. Add to casserole mixing with juices. Bake 15 minutes longer until heated and cheese is melted.

CLUB SALAD

Romaine, torn in bite-size pieces
1 avocado, sliced
1 tomato, sliced
6 mushrooms, sliced

Onion rings
Garlic croutons
Freshly grated Parmesan cheese

Mix romaine with dressing to moisten. Place on individual plates. Place 2 tomato slices on one side of the plate and avocado slices on the other. Add mushrooms and onion rings. Spread dressing on vegetables. Top with garlic croutons and Parmesan cheese to cover.

Dressing:

2 Tbs. white wine vinegar
2 Tbs. lemon juice
½ cup oil
1 clove garlic, minced
½ tsp. salt

¼ tsp. pepper
¾ tsp. sugar
½ tsp. dry mustard
¼ tsp. oregano

Combine all ingredients and mix well.

RASPBERRY GINGER CREAM

3 pkgs. (10 oz. each) frozen
   raspberries
1½ pints whipping cream

1 cup brown sugar, packed
½ tsp. ginger

Thaw and drain berries until separated but not dry, reserving juice. Whip cream until stiff. Mix brown sugar and ginger; add to cream. Fold in berries. Put in individual dishes. Top with a spoonful of juice. Chill several hours.

Olive Wrap-Ups

Rock Cornish Game Hens with
    Brown Rice and Nut Stuffing

Vegetable Saute

Tossed Green Salad

Feather Buns

Fruit with Creme Fraiche

Oregon or Washington White Riesling

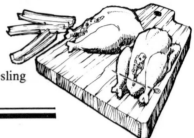

OLIVE WRAP-UPS

½ cup butter at room temperature
1 cup flour
½ tsp. salt
1 tsp. paprika

2 cups grated sharp Cheddar
* cheese*
1 jar (9½ oz.) pimiento-stuffed
* green olives, drained*

Mix butter with flour, salt and paprika in food processor. Add cheese and mix. Pinch off a small amount of dough and flatten in hand. Wrap around olive. Freeze. Do not thaw before baking. Bake 15 minutes at 400°.

ROCK CORNISH GAME HENS with BROWN RICE and NUT STUFFING

4 Cornish game hens
Salt and pepper
½ cup chopped onions
2 Tbs. butter
¼ cup chopped filberts or walnuts
3 Tbs. chopped parsley

2 cups cooked brown rice
½ tsp. salt
½ tsp. thyme
Butter
¼ cup vermouth or white wine

Rinse out cavity of game hens and drain. Season inside and out with salt and pepper. Cook onions in butter until soft. Add nuts and parsley and cook 1 minute. Add rice and seasonings. Stuff game hens with rice mixture. Place breast side up in buttered baking dish and rub with butter. Pour vermouth over. Bake 1 hour 15 minutes at 350°. Baste with drippings several times.

VEGETABLE SAUTE

½ head cauliflower, broken and trimmed
3 Tbs. butter
6-8 mushrooms
1 small onion, sliced

1 zucchini, sliced
1 cup fresh pea pods
Salt and pepper to taste
Parmesan cheese (optional)

Blanch cauliflower in boiling salted water 5 minutes. Drain under cold water. Saute onions in butter until soft. Add mushrooms, zucchini and pea pods and stir-cook 2-3 minutes. Add salt and pepper. Sprinkle with Parmesan cheese if desired. Vegetables should be tender-crisp.

Poultry

FEATHER BUNS

1 pkg. yeast
1 cup lukewarm water
3 eggs
½ cup sugar

½ cup shortening
1 tsp. salt
4 cups flour

Combine yeast and water; let stand until bubbly. Beat eggs slightly and add yeast. Cut shortening into sugar and salt. Blend in 3 cups flour; add egg mixture and work in 1 cup flour. Cover and let stand in refrigerator overnight. Divide dough into fourths. Roll each piece out to ⅛ inch thick. Cut triangles like a pie. Roll each triangle from large to small end. Place on greased cookie sheets and let rise 3 hours. Bake 12 minutes at 375°.

FRUIT with CREME FRAICHE

1 pint strawberries, hulled,
   slightly sweetened
2 oranges, sliced

1 cup seedless grapes
1 large banana, sliced

Combine fruit and serve with Creme Fraiche.

Creme Fraiche: (Make the day before)
1 cup whipping cream
2 Tbs. buttermilk

Combine in a jar with a lid. Shake well. Let stand at room temperature 8 hours. Refrigerate.

Buttermilk Chicken and Noodles

Carrots and Broccoli with Herb Butter

Fruit Salad with Pineapple Peanut Butter Dressing

Blueberry Muffins

Walnut Cookies

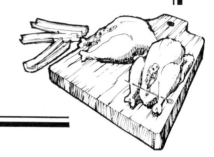

BUTTERMILK CHICKEN

1 fryer, cut up
½ cup flour
½ tsp. each salt and paprika
¼ tsp. pepper
1 Tbs. oil
2 Tbs. butter
½ cup chopped onion
1 can (1 lb.) whole tomatoes,
  broken up

1 cup buttermilk
½ tsp. salt
½ tsp. dillweed
2 Tbs. chopped fresh parsley
1 Tbs. flour
¼ cup water

Shake chicken in a paper bag with flour, salt, pepper and paprika. Reserve 1 Tbs. of remaining flour. Brown chicken in oil and butter. Add onions, tomatoes, buttermilk, salt and dillweed. Cover and bake at 350° for 50 minutes. Sprinkle with parsley. Uncover and cook 15 minutes longer. Remove excessive fat. If a thicker sauce is desired, add flour mixed with water and cook 5 minutes. Serve with hot noodles.

CARROTS and BROCCOLI with LEMON HERB BUTTER

2 carrots, cut in strips
2 cups broccoli flowerets
1 Tbs. fresh lemon juice

2 Tbs. butter, melted
½ tsp. salt
¼ tsp. fines herbes

Steam carrots 8 minutes. Add broccoli and cook 8-10 minutes longer. Combine lemon juice, butter and seasonings and toss with vegetables. Serves 4.

FRUIT SALAD

Fresh pineapple slices
Apple slices

Cantaloupe slices
Strawberries

Serve with Pineapple-Peanut Butter Dressing.

Pineapple-Peanut Butter Dressing:
½ cup pineapple juice
¼ cup peanut butter

⅔ cup oil

Blend pineapple juice and peanut butter in food processor or blender. With motor running, add oil slowly.

BLUEBERRY MUFFINS

1½ cups flour
½ cup sugar
2 tsp. baking powder
½ tsp. salt
¼ cup margarine, softened

1 egg
½ cup milk
1 cup fresh blueberries, washed
  and drained

Mix flour, sugar, baking powder and salt. Add margarine, egg and milk. Stir with a fork just until blended. Fold berries into batter carefully. Fill greased muffin cups ⅔ full. Bake 20-25 minutes at 400°.

WALNUT COOKIES

1 cup shortening or margarine
2 cups brown sugar
2 eggs
1½ cups buttermilk

3½ cups flour
1 tsp. baking soda
1 tsp. salt
1 cup chopped walnuts

Mix shortening, sugar and eggs. Add buttermilk. Sift flour, baking soda and salt together. Add to first mixture. Fold in walnuts. Chill dough. Drop by teaspoons on a lightly greased cookie sheet. Bake 8-10 minutes at 400°.

Beer Chicken

Filbert Rice Casserole

Green Beans with Parsley Butter

Patio Salad

Quick Rhubarb Cake

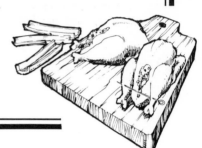

BEER CHICKEN

1 fryer, cut up
1 cup beer
½ cup soy sauce
1 Tbs. oil

2 cloves garlic, minced
1 Tbs. chopped onion
1 Tbs. chopped parsley

Marinate chicken in beer, soy, oil, garlic, onion and parsley several hours. Barbecue 1 hour turning and brushing with sauce frequently.

FILBERT RICE CASSEROLE

1 cup uncooked rice
1 cup water
1 cup beef broth
1 Tbs. soy sauce
2 tsp. Worcestershire sauce

¼ tsp. salt
⅛ tsp. pepper
¼ cup chopped filberts
2 Tbs. butter

Mix and place in greased casserole. Cover and bake 1 hour at 350° or until liquid is absorbed.

GREEN BEANS with PARSLEY BUTTER

1 lb. green beans, snapped
2-3 Tbs. butter
2 Tbs. chopped parsley

¼ tsp. salt
1 tsp. fresh lemon juice

Drop beans in a large kettle of salted boiling water. Boil 10-12 minutes. Drain and rinse under cold water to set color and texture. Melt butter in fry pan, add parsley and salt. Toss drained beans with butter mixture and lemon juice. Serve hot. Serves 4-5.

PATIO SALAD

Iceberg and romaine lettuce, torn
½ cup bean sprouts
2 tomatoes, cut up
3 green onions, sliced

1 cucumber, sliced
¼ cup garbanzo beans, drained
1 Tbs. sunflower seeds

Mix lettuce with bean sprouts, tomatoes, onions, cucumbers, garbanzo beans and dressing (page 93). Top with sunflower seeds.

QUICK RHUBARB CAKE

4 cups thinly sliced rhubarb
2 cups sugar
2 cups flour
1 tsp. salt
1½ tsp. baking soda

1 tsp. cinnamon
2 eggs, beaten
1 cup oil
1 cup chopped nuts (optional)

Place rhubarb in a buttered baking dish. Sprinkle with sugar. Let stand while sifting flour, salt, soda and cinnamon twice. Add to fruit. Add eggs, oil and nuts. Stir only until mixed. Bake 45-50 minutes at 350°.

Cheese Spread with Crackers

Barbecued Chicken

Bulgar Pilaf

Corn on the Cob

Tomatoes with Basil Dressing

Fresh Raspberries and Cream

Oregon Pinot Noir

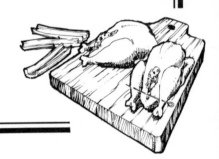

CHEESE SPREAD

3 cups grated sharp Cheddar
   cheese
2 cloves garlic, minced

½ tsp. dry mustard
1 tsp. Worcestershire sauce
¼ cup white wine

Blend all ingredients together in food processor. Chill several hours or overnight. Bring to room temperature before serving. Spread on crackers.

BARBECUED CHICKEN

1 or 2 fryers, cut up
Oil

Barbecue Sauce:
1 cup catsup
1 cup chili sauce
1 cup water
2 Tbs. cider vinegar
3 Tbs. brown sugar
1 Tbs. Worcestershire sauce

1 Tbs. Dijon-style mustard
1 tsp. salt
¼ tsp. pepper
1 Tbs. lemon juice
¼ cup chopped onion

Combine above ingredients and simmer 10 minutes.

Rub chicken with oil. Barbecue for 30 minutes. Brush with sauce and cook 30 minutes longer turning and basting several times.

BULGAR PILAF

1½ Tbs. butter	*2 cups chicken broth*
3 shallots, or green onions,	*½ tsp. salt*
chopped	*Pepper*
1 cup bulgar (cracked wheat)	*2 Tbs. chopped parsley*

Saute shallots and bulgar in butter until shallots are tender and bulgar is golden. Add broth, salt and pepper and bring to a boil. Cover and simmer 15-20 minutes. Add parsley and fluff with a fork.

Variations:
Add chopped ripe or green olives.
Add chopped nuts.
Add sauteed mushrooms.

TOMATOES with BASIL DRESSING

2-3 large tomatoes, sliced ¼ inch	*Freshly ground pepper*
thick	*Parsley sprigs*
1 mild onion, sliced	

Marinate tomato slices in dressing 1-2 hours.

Basil Dressing:

¼ cup olive oil	*½ tsp. sugar*
2 Tbs. red wine vinegar	*¼ cup fresh basil leaves or*
1 clove garlic, minced	*½ tsp. dried basil*
½ tsp. salt	

Blend all ingredients in a jar and shake well.

Arrange tomato and onion slices on a platter. Grind pepper on top. Pass extra dressing. Garnish with parsley sprigs.

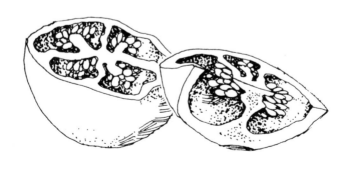

Barbecued Chicken in Spicy Wine Marinade

Idaho Potato Casserole

Green Beans

Marinated Carrots

Fresh Strawberry Sauce
and Ice Cream

BARBECUED CHICKEN in SPICY WINE MARINADE

1 fryer, cut in fourths
Marinate chicken for 1-2 hours.
Drain and barbecue 1 hour,
basting frequently.

Spicy Wine Marinade:

½ cup white wine
¼ cup oil
1 Tbs. white wine vinegar
1 tsp. salt

½ tsp. Italian seasoning
2 cloves garlic, minced
¼ tsp. pepper
1 Tbs. Dijon mustard

IDAHO POTATO CASSEROLE

5-6 potatoes (about 2 lbs.)
1/4 lb. grated Gruyere cheese
1/2 onion, sliced
1 cup sour cream
1/2 tsp. Dijon mustard

1/4 tsp. salt
2 Tbs. chopped parsley
1/4 cup grated Parmesan cheese
2 Tbs. butter
1/4 cup white wine

Cook unpeeled potatoes until tender, about 20 minutes. Rinse under cold water. Peel and slice. Mix sour cream, mustard, salt and parsley together. Layer potatoes, Gruyere, onion slices and sour cream mixture in buttered casserole. Repeat until all potatoes are used. Sprinkle Parmesan on top. Dot with butter. Pour wine over. Bake uncovered 30-35 minutes at 350° until bubbly.

MARINATED CARROTS

1 can (8 oz.) tomato sauce
1/2 cup sugar
1/4 cup oil
1/2 cup vinegar
1 Tbs. Worcestershire sauce
1/4 tsp. salt
1 tsp. prepared mustard

2 lbs. carrots, cooked and sliced in
   1/4-inch slices
1/2 green pepper, cut in pieces
   (optional)
1/2 onion, chopped
1 cup chopped celery

Mix tomato sauce, sugar, oil, vinegar, Worcestershire, salt and mustard. Heat and pour over carrots, green pepper, onion and celery. Chill at least 4 hours or overnight.

FRESH STRAWBERRY SAUCE

1 pint fresh strawberries, rinsed
   and hulled
1 Tbs. sugar
1 tsp. lemon juice

1 Tbs. orange-flavored liqueur
   (optional)
1 pint vanilla ice cream

Cut berries in half and put into a small bowl. Sprinkle with sugar and lemon juice and coarsely mash with a fork. Cover and let stand at room temperature for 1-3 hours. Before serving add liqueur. Serve over ice cream.

Oregon Cheese Ball

Summerset Chicken

Zucchini Stuffed with Spinach

Tossed Salad

Garlic Toast

Gooseberry Fool

Oregon White Riesling

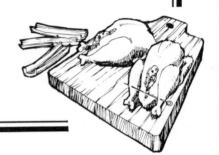

OREGON CHEESE BALL

8 oz. cream cheese
¼ lb. Oregon Cheddar cheese
½ oz. Roquefort cheese
¼ cup mayonnaise

1 Tbs. grated onion
1 clove garlic, crushed
2 tsp. Worcestershire sauce
Chopped filberts

Mix cheeses in food processor. Add remaining ingredients except nuts. Form in 2 balls. Roll in nuts. Chill. Bring to room temperature before serving.

SUMMERSET CHICKEN

1 fryer, cut up
¼ tsp. salt
¼ cup flour
2 Tbs. butter
1 Tbs. oil
⅔ cup chicken broth
1 clove garlic, minced

¼ tsp. each oregano and paprika
⅛ tsp. rosemary
¼ tsp. salt
1 cup mushrooms, sliced
1 Tbs. cornstarch
1 Tbs. water

Coat chicken with flour and salt. Brown on all sides in oil and butter. Pour off excess oil. Add chicken broth. Stir to loosen browned bits. Add garlic and seasonings. Cover and simmer 1 hour. Add mushrooms and cook 10 minutes longer. Blend cornstarch with water. Stir into broth until thickened.

ZUCCHINI STUFFED with SPINACH

6 small zucchini (allow 1 zucchini
  per person)
1 onion, chopped
1 clove garlic, minced
½ cup chopped mushrooms
1½ Tbs. butter
1 pkg. (10 oz.) frozen chopped
  spinach, thawed and squeeze
  drained

¼ cup dry bread crumbs
2 Tbs. Parmesan cheese
½ tsp. salt
¼ tsp. pepper
2 eggs, beaten
1½ cups grated jack cheese

Cook zucchini in salted water 8 minutes. Remove and cut in half lengthwise. When cool enough to handle, scrape out centers and chop. Saute onion, garlic and mushrooms in butter. Add zucchini pulp and spinach. Stir to mix. Add crumbs, Parmesan cheese, salt and pepper and blend. Add eggs and mix. Fill centers of zucchini and cover the top. Bake 15 minutes at 350°. Top with jack cheese and bake 5 minutes longer.

GOOSEBERRY FOOL

2 pints gooseberries, remove
  stems and blossom

¾ cup sugar
1 cup whipping cream, whipped

Place gooseberries in a saucepan with sugar and cook for about 15 minutes or until soft. Press through a sieve. Cool. Mix gooseberries with whipped cream and refrigerate until serving time. Makes 6 servings.

Country Chicken Stew

Noodles

Fruit Salad

Big Cookies

COUNTRY CHICKEN STEW

1 fryer, cut up
¼ cup flour
1 tsp. salt
¼ tsp. pepper
2 Tbs. butter
2 Tbs. oil
6 tiny onions
4 carrots, cut in thirds

1 can (16 oz.) whole tomatoes,
  pureed
½ cup red wine
½ tsp. thyme
1 bay leaf
6-8 mushrooms, quartered
½ tsp. salt or to taste

Shake chicken in a bag with flour, salt and pepper. Reserve left-over flour mixture. Melt butter and oil in pan and brown chicken on all sides. Add onions, carrots, tomatoes, wine, thyme and bay leaf. Cover and bake 45 minutes at 350°. Add mushrooms and bake 15 minutes longer. Mix left-over flour with ¼ cup water. Add to casserole and mix. Taste for seasoning and add salt if necessary. Remove bay leaf before serving.

BIG COOKIES

1½ cups shortening   1½ cups granulated sugar
1½ cups brown sugar

Cream above ingredients and add:
4 eggs   1 tsp. baking powder
2 tsp. vanilla   1 tsp. nutmeg
1 tsp. salt   2 tsp. cinnamon
1 tsp. baking soda

By hand add: *(Batter will be stiff)*
3 cups white flour   2 cups coconut
1 cup whole wheat flour   2 cups raisins
2 cups quick cooking oats   2 cups chopped nuts
2 cups wheat germ

Drop by spoonsful on greased cookie sheet and bake 15 minutes at 350°.

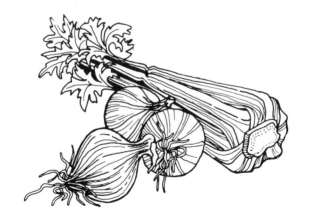

Roast Turkey

Orange Glazed Sweet Potatoes

Whipped Potatoes

Peas and Onions

Cranberry Mold or Sauce

Pumpkin Spice Bars

Oregon or Washington Gewurztraminer

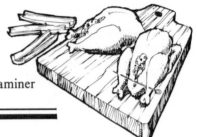

ROAST TURKEY

Rub oil on turkey and stuff with your favorite dressing. Roast 20 minutes to the pound at 325°. Cover with foil if turkey becomes too brown.

Note: For a quick and easy stuffing, sprinkle cavity with salt and sage. Add 2 onions, quartered, and 2 celery stalks. Especially good for barbecuing.

ORANGE GLAZED SWEET POTATOES

6-8 sweet potatoes or yams,
  unpeeled
Salt
4 Tbs. butter
3 Tbs. brown sugar OR
  2 Tbs. honey

½ tsp. salt
2 tsp. orange peel
1 cup orange juice

Cook potatoes in boiling salted water until almost tender, about 15 minutes. Drain and cool. Peel and cut in half lengthwise. Cut each half crosswise. Arrange in greased baking dish. Melt butter; add sugar, salt, peel and juice. Pour over potatoes and bake 30 minutes at 350°. Serves 8.

CRANBERRY SAUCE

3 cups cranberries
2 cups boiling water

2 cups sugar
3 strips orange peel

Wash and pick over cranberries. Place in large pan; add water, sugar and orange peel. Boil 10 minutes.

CRANBERRY MOLD

1 Tbs. unflavored gelatin
3 Tbs. water
2 cups cranberries, washed and
   sorted
1 cup boiling water or orange juice

½ cup sugar
¼ tsp. salt
¾ cup chopped celery
1 cup chopped apples
½ cup walnuts, coarsely chopped

Soften gelatin in 3 Tbs. water. Cook cranberries in 1 cup water or juice until skins pop. Add sugar and salt and cook 5 minutes longer. Add gelatin and mix well. Chill until slightly set. Fold in celery, apples and walnuts and chill until firm.

PUMPKIN SPICE BARS

4 eggs, slightly beaten
¾ cup salad oil
2 cups sugar
1 can (1 lb.) pumpkin
¾ tsp. salt
2 tsp. cinnamon

¼ tsp. ginger
¾ tsp. cloves
½ tsp. nutmeg
2 tsp. baking powder
1 tsp. baking soda
2 cups all-purpose flour

Combine eggs, oil, sugar and pumpkin; beat and blend well. Stir together salt, cinnamon, ginger, cloves, nutmeg, baking powder, baking soda and flour. Add to pumpkin mixture and beat well. Pour into greased 9x13 baking pan and bake 25-30 minutes at 350°. When cool, spread with Cream Cheese Frosting.

Cream Cheese Frosting:

3 oz. cream cheese, room
   temperature
3 Tbs. butter or margarine,
   softened

2 tsp. orange juice
1 tsp. vanilla
1¾-2 cups confectioners' sugar

Beat cheese and butter together until fluffy. Add orange juice, vanilla and sugar (small amounts at a time until desired consistency). Beat well.

Meats

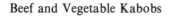

Beef and Vegetable Kabobs

Barbecued Beans

Tossed Salad with Creamy Garlic Dressing

French Bread

First Prize Vanilla Ice Cream

BEEF and VEGETABLE KABOBS

*1 top sirloin, 1 inch thick (about
    1¼ lbs.) cut in 1¼-inch pieces
6-8 mushroom caps of uniform
    size*

*2 zucchini, cut in ½-inch slices
1 small onion, cut in pieces
1 green pepper, cut in pieces*

Marinate beef in marinade (page 92) for 3 hours, turning several times.
Thread beef and vegetables on skewers. Place on grill (barbecue or stove
top) and cook about 12-15 minutes turning frequently and basting with
marinade. Serves 4.

Variation: Use Barbecue Sauce (page 78).

BARBECUE BEANS

5 slices bacon, diced
2 onions, sliced
1 can (1 lb.) red kidney beans,
    drained
1 can (1 lb.) baby limas, drained
2 cans (1 lb. each) pork and beans,
    undrained

1 clove garlic, minced
1 Tbs. brown sugar
1 Tbs. vinegar
1 Tbs. prepared mustard
1 tsp. Worcestershire
3 oz. tomato paste (½ small can)

Cook bacon and set aside. Saute onion rings in bacon fat. Remove with slotted spoon. Combine onions and bacon with remaining ingredients and mix well. Bake uncovered 1 hour at 350°.

CREAMY GARLIC DRESSING

½ cup mayonnaise
¼ cup sour cream
2 cloves garlic, minced
1 Tbs. lemon juice

1 tsp. Worcestershire sauce
½ tsp. salt
3 Tbs. Parmesan cheese
2 Tbs. milk

Mix all ingredients well.

FIRST PRIZE VANILLA ICE CREAM

2¼ cups sugar
6 Tbs. flour
½ tsp. salt
5 cups light cream, scalded

6 eggs, beaten
4 cups whipping cream
5 tsp. vanilla

Combine sugar, flour and salt. Slowly add light cream. Stir-cook over medium-low heat 10 minutes until mixture begins to thicken. Mix small amount of hot mixture into beaten eggs; then add all to eggs. Chill. Add whipping cream and vanilla. Place in ice cream freezer container and follow directions.

Beef Barbecue with Two Marinades

Cheesy Potatoes in Foil

Marinated Vegetable Platter

Rhubarb Crisp

Oregon Cabernet Sauvignon

BEEF BARBECUE with TWO MARINADES
(Choose one):

Top round, 2-2½ inches thick (about 3 lbs.)

WINE MARINADE:

¾ cup red wine
¼ cup soy sauce
2 Tbs. lemon juice
1 Tbs. oil

2 cloves garlic, minced
½ tsp. salt
½ tsp. each ginger and dry
  mustard

BEER MARINADE:

1 cup beer
½ cup catsup
1 Tbs. lemon juice
½ cup chopped onion

1 Tbs. Worcestershire sauce
¾ tsp. salt
Dash Tabasco

Mix marinade ingredients. Poke holes with a fork on both sides of meat. Pour marinade over. Let stand 3-4 hours. Turn several times. Remove steak from marinade and barbecue 45-50 minutes. Turn several times and brush with marinade while cooking. Serves 6.

Note: Sprinkle with unseasoned meat tenderizer before adding marinade for more tender results.

CHEESY POTATOES in FOIL

4 potatoes unpeeled and cut into
   ¼-inch slices
1 medium onion, minced or sliced
4 Tbs. butter or margarine, cut
   into small pieces
1 tsp. salt

¼ tsp. pepper
¼ tsp. caraway seeds
1 cup grated sharp Cheddar
   cheese
2 Tbs. milk

Divide ingredients on two sheets of heavy duty foil. Seal tightly. Lay on grill and cook 50-60 minutes. Turn several times.

MARINATED VEGETABLE PLATTER

1-2 cucumbers, sliced
2 tomatoes, cut in wedges
1 green pepper, cut in strips
1 cup sliced celery
4 green onions, sliced

6-8 mushrooms, sliced
½ cup sliced radishes
½ cup garbanzo beans
8 ripe olives
1 cup Swiss cheese, cubed

Arrange vegetables on platter. Spoon dressing on vegetables 2 hours before serving. Chill. Add olives and cheese. Pass extra Dressing.

Dressing:
½ cup oil
2 Tbs. red wine vinegar
1 clove garlic, minced
¼ tsp. oregano
⅛ tsp. basil

1 Tbs. chopped parsley
½ tsp. salt
¼ tsp. paprika
Freshly grated pepper

Mix well.

RHUBARB CRISP

6 cups sliced rhubarb
1½ cups sugar
2 Tbs. water
1 cup flour

½ tsp. cinnamon
⅛ tsp. salt
½ cup butter

Combine rhubarb, 1 cup sugar and water in baking dish. Combine flour, remaining sugar, cinnamon and salt. Add butter and mix with pastry blender until mixture is crumbly. Sprinkle over rhubarb. Bake 50 minutes at 350° until bubbly. Serve warm or cold.

Cafe Steaks with Shallot Butter

Mushroom Casserole

Green Beans

Spinach Salad

Cheese and Fruit

Irish Coffee

Washington Cabernet Sauvignon

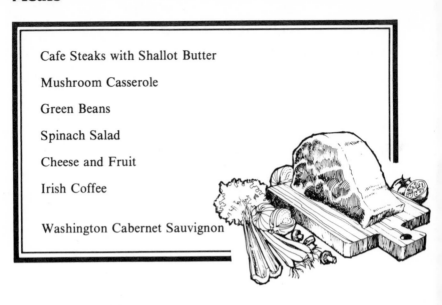

CAFE STEAKS

4 T-bones or New York steaks

Broil or barbecue to desired doneness. Top with Shallot Butter.

Shallot Butter:

½ cup chopped shallots or green onions
¼ cup butter

2 cloves garlic, crushed
¹/3 cup chopped parsley

Saute shallots in butter. Add garlic and cook briefly. Add parsley.

MUSHROOM CASSEROLE

2 lbs. mushrooms, sliced
1 cup butter
5 green onions, sliced
2 Tbs. flour
1 cup sour cream
2 Tbs. chopped parsley

½ tsp. salt
½ tsp. lemon pepper
3 slices fresh white bread, made into crumbs
2 tsp. butter

Saute mushrooms and onions in 1 cup butter until slightly tender (about 3 minutes). Add flour and stir. Add sour cream, parsley and seasonings. Place in casserole. Cover with crumbs. Melt 2 tsp. butter and pour over. Bake uncovered 30 minutes at 350°.

SPINACH SALAD

*2 bunches fresh spinach, washed
  and torn*
*6-8 slices bacon, cooked and
  crumbled*

6 green onions, sliced
2-3 hard-cooked eggs, chopped

Toss with dressing to coat.

Dressing:
1 clove garlic, minced
1/4 cup white wine vinegar
1 Tbs. water
*1 tsp. each soy sauce and
  Worcestershire sauce*
1 tsp. sugar

1 tsp. dry mustard
1/4-1/2 tsp. curry powder
1/2 tsp. salt
Freshly ground pepper
2/3 cup vegetable oil

Mix and shake well in a covered jar.

CHEESE and FRUIT

Blue Cheese
Camembert or Brie
Cheddar

Serve with fruit.
Pears, apples and grapes

IRISH COFFEE

Strong coffee
1 tsp. brown sugar for each cup
1 jigger whiskey for each cup

*Whipping cream, whipped and
  slightly sweetened*

Meats

Artichoke Dip

Roast Sirloin of Beef

Mushroom Stuffed Potatoes

French Onions

Tossed Salad with Green Dressing

Washington Walnut Pie

Washington Cabernet Sauvignon

ARTICHOKE DIP

1 can (8½ oz.) artichokes, drained   *1 cup mayonnaise*
  (not marinated)   *1 cup grated Parmesan cheese*

Mix in food processor and bake 20 minutes at 350°. Serve with chips or
raw vegetables.

ROAST SIRLOIN of BEEF

3½-4 lbs. beef sirloin   *1 tsp. salt*
1 clove garlic, crushed   *½ tsp. pepper*
1 tsp. dry mustard

Combine garlic, mustard, salt and pepper and rub on beef. Place roast,
fat side up, in roasting pan. Roast uncovered at 325° for 1¼ hours for
rare; or 2-2½ hours for medium. Let roast stand 10 minutes on heated
platter for easier carving. Slice thinly on the diagonal.

Gravy:
¼ cup meat drippings   *2 cups beef broth*
3 Tbs. flour   *Dash of pepper*

Stir flour into drippings until smooth, loosening any browned bits in the
pan. Stir broth into flour mixture. Add pepper and stir constantly until
thickened. Add salt to taste.

MUSHROOM STUFFED POTATOES

4 baking potatoes
1 tsp. salt
1/4 tsp. pepper
1/3-1/2 cup milk, warmed

1 cup mushrooms, chopped
2 Tbs. chopped green onion
2 Tbs. butter
1 tsp. lemon juice

Wash potatoes and bake 40-50 minutes at 425°. Slit potatoes and scoop the pulp into a bowl. Add salt, pepper and milk and beat with rotary beater until fluffy. Saute mushrooms and onion in butter and lemon juice. Add to potato mixture and mix well. Spoon back into shells. Bake 15 minutes longer at 350°.

FRENCH ONIONS

4 large onions, sliced
3 Tbs. butter
2 Tbs. flour
Dash pepper
3/4 cup rich beef broth
1/4 cup dry sherry

1 1/2 cups plain croutons
2 Tbs. butter, melted
1/2 cup Swiss or Gruyere cheese,
*   shredded*
3 Tbs. Parmesan cheese

Cook onions in 3 Tbs. butter just until tender. Blend in flour and pepper. Add broth and sherry; cook and stir until thickened and bubbly. Turn into 1-quart casserole. Toss croutons with 2 Tbs. melted butter and spoon on top of onion mixture. Sprinkle with Swiss and Parmesan cheeses. Place under broiler just until cheese melts, about 1 minute. Serve immediately.

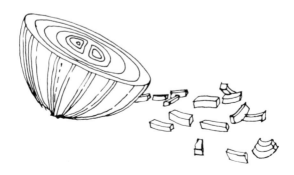

GREEN DRESSING

¹/₃ cup parsley
2 green onions, cut in fourths
1 clove garlic
1 egg yolk
1 Tbs. fresh lemon juice

1 Tbs. white wine vinegar
¹/₂ tsp. salt
¹/₂ tsp. dry mustard
1 cup oil

Chop parsley, onion and garlic in food processor. Add yolk, lemon juice, vinegar, salt and mustard and blend. With machine running, slowly add oil in a thin, steady stream until thickened.

WASHINGTON WALNUT PIE

3 eggs, well beaten
¹/₂ cup brown sugar
Dash of salt
1 cup light corn syrup

¹/₄ cup butter, melted
1 cup chopped walnuts
9-inch unbaked pie crust
Whipped cream

Mix first six ingredients and pour into pie shell. Bake 50 minutes at 350°. Serve with whipped cream.

Pork Roast with Vegetables

Squash Casserole

Fruit Salad

Chunky Apple Sauce

Hot Rolls

Buttermilk Brownie Cake

Oregon Rose of Pinot Noir

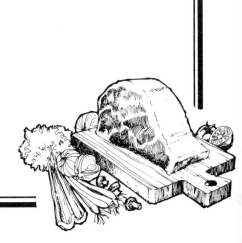

PORK ROAST with VEGETABLES

3-4 lb. pork roast
3 potatoes, cut in half

4 carrots, cut in large chunks
2 apples, quartered

Rub roast with Marinade 4 hours before baking time. Bake 30 minutes to the pound at 325°. Add potatoes and carrots last hour of cooking time. Add apples last ½ hour of cooking time.

Marinade:
3 large cloves garlic, minced
1 tsp. salt
½ tsp. each rosemary and thyme

⅛ tsp. allspice
3 Tbs. oil
Freshly ground pepper

Combine and mix well.

Meats

SQUASH CASSEROLE

*1½-2 lbs. zucchini or crookneck
squash, or combination,
unpeeled
3 green onions, sliced
3 Tbs. melted butter
¼ tsp. salt*

*¼ tsp. white pepper
½ cup sour cream
¼ cup dry bread crumbs
¾ cup Cheddar cheese
Parmesan cheese*

Cut squash into bite-size pieces about ¾ inch thick. Steam 5 minutes. Drain for 5 minutes. Place in casserole and mix with onions, butter, salt, pepper and sour cream. Add bread crumbs and cheeses. Bake uncovered 10 minutes at 350°.

CHUNKY APPLESAUCE

*8 cups coarsely chopped, pared
cooking apples
1/3-½ cup water or wine*

*1/3 cup packed brown sugar
½ tsp. cinnamon
½ cup coarsely chopped walnuts*

Combine apples and water or wine in a 3-quart saucepan. Cover and cook over high heat until mixture comes to a boil, about 2 minutes. Simmer 10-12 minutes or until apples are very tender, stirring occasionally. Stir in brown sugar and cinnamon. Cook 2 minutes. Remove from heat and mash with a vegetable masher. Fold in walnuts.

Note: For smooth applesauce, puree in food processor.

BUTTERMILK BROWNIE CAKE

1 cup water	*1 tsp. baking soda*
1 cup butter	*1 tsp. cinnamon*
¼ cup cocoa	*2 eggs*
2 cups flour	*½ cup buttermilk*
2 cups sugar	*½ tsp. vanilla*

Blend water, butter and cocoa in saucepan; heat to boiling. Mix flour, sugar, soda and cinnamon. Add cocoa mixture and blend well. Stir in the eggs and buttermilk and beat well. Pour into a greased 15½x10½ jelly roll pan. Bake for 20 minutes at 400°. Spread with frosting while still hot.

Chocolate Frosting:

⅓ cup buttermilk	*1 lb. confectioners' sugar*
½ cup butter	*1 cup chopped nuts*
¼ cup cocoa	

Heat buttermilk and butter together to boiling. Pour over the sugar and cocoa and beat until creamy. Add nuts.

Salmon Pate

Sour Cream Pork Chops

Herbed Asparagus

Fluffy Rice

Romaine Bacon Apple Salad

Cranberry Sherbet

Oregon Pinot Noir

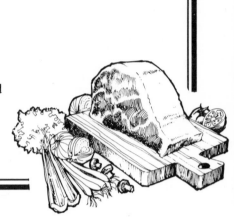

SALMON PATE

1 can (16 oz.) salmon
8 oz. cream cheese, softened
1 Tbs. grated onion
2 Tbs. lemon juice
1 tsp. horseradish

1 tsp. Worcestershire sauce
1/4 tsp. salt
1/2 cup chopped pecans
Chopped parsley

Drain and flake salmon. Remove bones and skin. Combine with cheese, onion, lemon juice, horseradish, Worcestershire and salt. Shape in a mound on a plate. Sprinkle with pecans and parsley. Chill. Serve with crackers.

SOUR CREAM PORK CHOPS

6 pork chops, 1 inch thick
Sage
Salt and pepper
1 Tbs. oil
1 onion, sliced

1/2 cup chicken broth
1/4 cup white wine
1/2 cup sour cream
2 tsp. flour
Chopped parsley

Sprinkle pork chops with sage, salt and pepper. Brown in oil. Add onion and stir-cook one minute. Add broth and wine. Cover and simmer 20 minutes. Remove chops from skillet. Combine sour cream and flour. Add to pan and stir until smooth. Return chops to pan and heat. Sprinkle with parsley.

ROMAINE BACON APPLE SALAD

See page 11.

HERBED ASPARAGUS

3 lbs. fresh asparagus
1 tsp. salt
3 Tbs. butter

1 Tbs. lemon juice
¼ tsp. basil

Clean and cut off tough ends of asparagus. Steam in salted water until tender. Drain. Melt butter and mix with lemon juice and basil. Pour over asparagus. Serves 6.

CRANBERRY SHERBET

4 cups cranberries
2 cups water

1 envelope unflavored gelatin
½ cup sugar

Cook cranberries in water until they pop. Add gelatin and sugar and stir. Puree in food processor. Cool and add syrup.

Syrup:
2 cups sugar
1 cup water

1 cup orange juice
Juice of 1 lemon

Boil sugar and water 5 minutes. When cool add juices. Add to cranberries. Freeze in baking dish several hours until almost firm. Place in food processor and blend. Return to baking dish and refreeze.

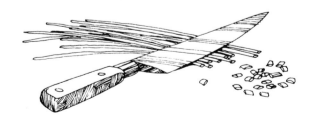

Teriyaki Flank Steak

Plank Potatoes

Baked Walla Walla Onions

Tomato and Avocado Salad with
Fresh Mayonnaise

Garlic Bread

Apples with Cheese Spread

Oregon Pinot Noir

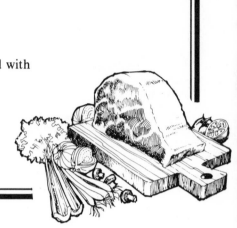

TERIYAKI FLANK STEAK

1-1½ lbs. flank steak
½ cup soy sauce
¼ cup white wine
2 cloves garlic, minced

½ tsp. ginger
¼ tsp. dry mustard
1 Tbs. sugar

Combine marinade ingredients and pour over flank steak. Marinate for 4-6 hours. Drain and barbecue 6 minutes on each side. Brush with marinade. Cut thin slices diagonally.

PLANK POTATOES

4 potatoes, scrubbed and sliced
*   lengthwise, 3/8" thick*
Oil
½ cup butter, melted

1 clove garlic
¼ tsp. salt
⅛ tsp. pepper

Brush both sides of potato slices with oil. Place on grill and cook 12-15 minutes. Turn with tongs. Brush with butter mixed with garlic, salt and pepper. Cook 10 minutes longer or until tender.

BAKED WALLA WALLA ONIONS

4 onions, peeled   *Nutmeg*
Butter

Cut an X on the top of each onion. Add butter and dash of nutmeg. Wrap tightly in foil. Bake in covered barbecue 1 hour turning several times.

Note: May also be baked in oven at 350°.

TOMATO and AVOCADO SALAD with FRESH MAYONNAISE

2 tomatoes, sliced   *1 onion, sliced*
2 avocados, sliced   *Parsley sprigs*

Alternate tomatoes, avocado slices and onion on a large platter surrounding a dish of Fresh Mayonnaise. Garnish with parsley.

Fresh Mayonnaise:
1 egg   *¼ tsp. salt*
1 Tbs. lemon juice or white wine   *¼ tsp. Italian herbs*
  vinegar   *1 cup oil*
1 Tbs. Dijon mustard

Blend egg, lemon juice, mustard, salt, herbs and 1 Tbs. oil in food processor or blender. With the motor running, add oil by drops. As mayonnaise thickens add oil in a steady stream. Refrigerate.

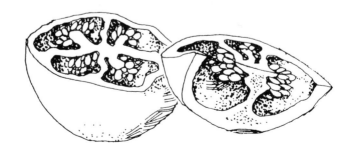

GARLIC BREAD

1 loaf French bread
½ cup butter
2 cloves garlic, minced

Parmesan cheese
Chopped parsley

Split bread lengthwise. Cut slices nearly to the bottom of the loaf. Mix butter with garlic and spread on cut sides of bread. Sprinkle with Parmesan cheese and parsley. Wrap in foil and bake 15 minutes at 350°.

APPLES with CHEESE SPREAD

8 oz. cream cheese
Milk
½ cup chopped filberts

½ cup chopped dates
1 can (8¼ oz.) crushed pineapple,
* drained*

Beat cream cheese until fluffy. Add a few drops of milk for desired consistency. Add nuts, dates and pineapple. Serve in a bowl surrounded with apple slices. Spread cheese mixture on apple slices.

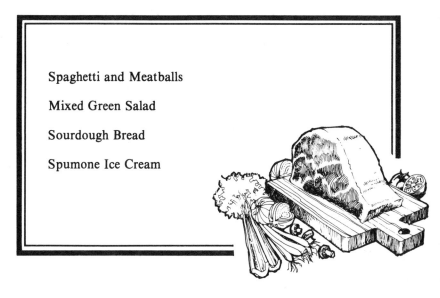

Spaghetti and Meatballs

Mixed Green Salad

Sourdough Bread

Spumone Ice Cream

SPAGHETTI and MEATBALLS

1 lb. spaghetti

Meatballs:

1½ lbs. ground beef　　　　　　*1 Tbs. chopped parsley*
2 eggs　　　　　　　　　　　　*1 Tbs. Parmesan cheese*
¾ cup fine dry bread crumbs　　*¼ tsp. each salt and pepper*

Mix well and refrigerate while making sauce.

Sauce:

1 onion, chopped　　　　　　　　*1 tsp. basil*
2 cloves garlic, minced　　　　　*1 tsp. oregano*
1 can (28 oz.) whole tomatoes,　　*¼ cup chopped parsley*
　broken up　　　　　　　　　　*¼ cup red wine*
1 can (1 lb.) tomato sauce　　　　*Freshly ground pepper*
1 tsp. salt

Combine and simmer several hours. Shape balls and bake 15 minutes at 375°. Add to sauce last ½ hour. Serve on cooked spaghetti.

Clam Dip

Barbecued Ribs, Northwest Style

Broccoli and Noodle Casserole

Cole Slaw

Garlic Bread

Fresh Peach Streusel

Oregon Merlot

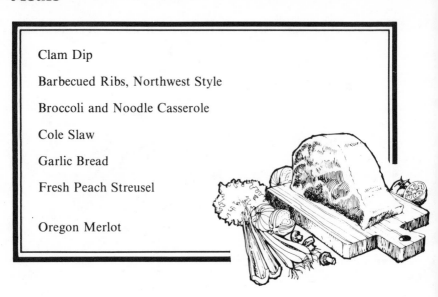

CLAM DIP

8 oz. cream cheese at room
temperature
1 can (7 oz.) minced clams,
drained, reserving liquid
1 clove garlic, minced

1 tsp. Worcestershire sauce
2 tsp. lemon juice
3 Tbs. clam juice
¼ tsp. salt

Beat cheese and combine with remaining ingredients. Chill several hours before serving.

BARBECUED RIBS, NORTHWEST STYLE

4-5 lbs. meaty pork spareribs, cut
in serving-size pieces

½ onion, cut in rings

Bake ribs and onion for 1 hour at 350°. Pour off grease. Add sauce (page 78) and bake or barbecue ½ hour longer.

BROCCOLI and NOODLE CASSEROLE

1½ lbs. fresh broccoli
½ cup chopped onion
1 clove garlic, minced
2 Tbs. butter
3 Tbs. flour
1¼ cups milk
2 Tbs. chopped fresh parsley
½ tsp. salt
¼ tsp. pepper
½ tsp. oregano
1½ cups creamed small curd
 cottage cheese
8 oz. noodles, cooked and drained
1 cup shredded Cheddar cheese
¼ cup grated Romano cheese

Cook broccoli in salted water 8 minutes. Refresh under cold water and drain. Set aside. In a saucepan cook onion and garlic in butter until soft. Stir in flour; add milk and stir until thickened. Remove from heat and add parsley, salt, pepper and oregano. Fold in cottage cheese. Combine sauce and broccoli with noodles in a greased baking dish. Sprinkle with cheeses. Bake 30 minutes at 350°.

COLESLAW

1 small head cabbage, sliced or
 chopped

Dressing:
½ cup mayonnaise or salad
 dressing*
½ cup sour cream
1 Tbs. vinegar
1 Tbs. sugar

¼ tsp. dill weed
½ tsp. salt
¼ tsp. seasoning salt
⅛ tsp. pepper

Combine all ingredients. Mix with cabbage about 2 hours before serving.

*Use freshly made mayonnaise (page 105) for best results.

Vegetable Slaw:

Add:

½ green pepper, diced
2 carrots, grated

1 celery rib, chopped
3 green onions, chopped

Omit dill weed and add ¼ tsp. caraway seeds or celery seeds.

FRESH PEACH STREUSEL

½ cup light brown sugar, packed
½ cup unsifted flour
½ cup butter
5-6 ripe peaches, peeled and sliced
¼ cup granulated sugar

½ tsp. nutmeg
1 egg
2 Tbs. light cream
1 tsp. vanilla

Combine brown sugar and flour; mix well. With pastry blender, cut in butter until mixture resembles coarse crumbs. Sprinkle ½ cup crumb mixture over bottom of pie pan. Add peaches. Sprinkle with granulated sugar and nutmeg. Beat together egg, light cream and vanilla. Pour over peaches. Cover with remaining crumb mixture. Bake 40-50 minutes at 375°. Serve warm with ice cream. Serves 6.

Open Face Reubens

Fruit Salad

Relishes

Chocolate-Walnut Clusters

Northwest Beer

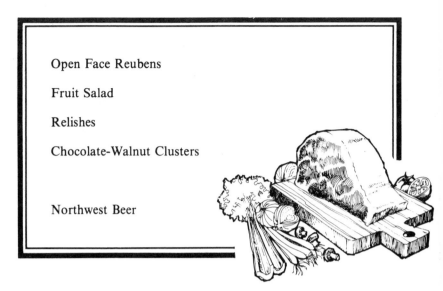

OPEN FACE REUBENS

¹/₄ cup mayonnaise
1¹/₂ tsp. horseradish
¹/₈ tsp. dry mustard
1 can (1 lb.) sauerkraut, well
  drained

Thinly sliced corned beef
¹/₃ cup sour cream
Swiss cheese slices
4-6 slices rye bread
3-4 Tbs. butter

Mix sour cream, mayonnaise, horseradish and mustard. Spread dressing on bread. Add beef, sauerkraut and cheese. Place sandwiches in melted butter in fry pan. Cover and cook slowly until bread is brown and cheese is melted, about 10 minutes.

CHOCOLATE-WALNUT CLUSTERS

¹/₂ cup flour
¹/₄ tsp. baking powder
¹/₄ tsp. salt
¹/₄ cup butter
¹/₂ cup sugar
1 large egg

1¹/₂ tsp. vanilla
1¹/₂ squares semi-sweet chocolate,
  melted
1³/₄ cups coarsely chopped
  walnuts

Sift flour, baking powder and salt together. Mix butter and sugar until creamy. Add egg and vanilla. Add chocolate and flour mixture. Fold in nuts. Drop by teaspoonfuls on greased cookie sheet. Bake 10 minutes at 350°.

Baked Ham with Orange Glaze

Sweet Potato Souffle

Buttered Broccoli

Rodeway Salad

Holiday Cake

Oregon Rose of Pinot Noir

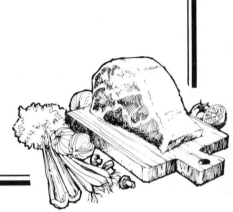

BAKED HAM with ORANGE GLAZE

1 fully cooked ham
6 oz. frozen orange juice
  concentrate
¼ cup packed brown sugar

1 tsp. dry mustard
1 tsp. Worcestershire sauce
Whole cloves (optional)

Bake ham one hour at 350°. Thaw orange juice concentrate and beat until smooth with brown sugar, mustard and Worcestershire. About 30 minutes before ham is done, remove from oven and score surface by cutting through fat in diamond shapes. Brush generously with orange glaze. Stud with whole cloves. Bake 30 minutes longer, brushing two or three times with remaining glaze. Let ham stand 15 minutes before slicing.

SWEET POTATO SOUFFLE

4 lbs. sweet potatoes, cooked
½ cup melted butter
6 eggs, separated
⅔ cup sugar

½ cup milk
1 Tbs. lemon rind
1 tsp. ginger
½ tsp. salt

Mash sweet potatoes. Add butter. Add yolks and beat until blended. Add sugar, milk, lemon rind, ginger and salt. Beat egg whites until stiff but not dry. Fold into potato mixture. Bake in a buttered 2-quart souffle dish for 1 hour at 325°.

RODEWAY SALAD

*1 head romaine, torn into bite-size
     pieces
6-8 mushrooms*

*4 green onions, sliced
6 slices bacon, cooked and cubed*

Dressing:

*²/₃ cup oil
¹/₄ cup white wine vinegar
1 clove garlic, minced
¹/₂ tsp. Tabasco*

*¹/₂ tsp. salt
1 tsp. dry mustard
1 tsp. paprika*

Mix in a jar and shake well.

HOLIDAY CAKE

*2¹/₄ cups all-purpose flour
1 cup sugar
1 tsp. baking soda
1¹/₂ cups fresh cranberries,
     coarsely chopped
1 cup chopped pitted dates*

*1 cup chopped walnuts
2 beaten eggs
1 cup buttermilk
³/₄ cup cooking oil
1 Tbs. finely shredded orange peel*

Stir together flour, sugar and soda. Add cranberries, dates and nuts. Combine eggs, buttermilk, oil and orange peel; add to flour mixture and mix well. Turn batter into greased and floured Bundt pan. Bake for 50-55 minutes at 350°. Cool in pan 30 minutes. Remove from pan onto wire rack. While warm, spoon on the Glaze.

Glaze:
*¹/₂ cup orange juice
³/₄ cup sugar*

Combine orange juice and sugar in small saucepan. Cook and stir until sugar dissolves.

Note: May use canned whole cranberry sauce, drained.

This cake keeps well.

Shrimp-Cucumber Spread

Veal with Herb-Lemon Sauce

Rice and Parsley

Zucchini Boats

Greek Salad

Walnut Tarts

Oregon Pinot Noir

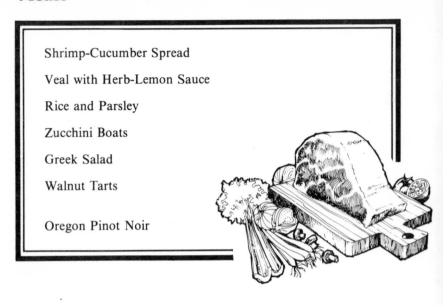

SHRIMP-CUCUMBER SPREAD

3 oz. cream cheese
2 Tbs. mayonnaise
1 cup small cooked shrimp
1 Tbs. catsup
1 tsp. mustard

1 clove garlic, minced
1 tsp. finely chopped onion
½ cucumber, cut up
Rye rounds or crackers

Blend all ingredients except crackers in food processor until smooth.

VEAL with HERB-LEMON SAUCE

8 veal scallops (about 1½ lbs.)
Salt and pepper
⅓ cup flour
¼ cup butter
1 Tbs. oil
2 Tbs. white wine

½ cup chicken broth
2 Tbs. lemon juice
1 cup sliced mushrooms
2 green onions, chopped
1 Tbs. minced parsley
½ tsp. dried rosemary

Salt and pepper veal. Dip in flour. Melt butter with oil and brown veal quickly on both sides turning frequently. Transfer veal to warm platter. Add wine, broth, lemon juice, mushrooms, onions, parsley and rosemary to pan. Reduce heat. Simmer 3-5 minutes. Return veal to skillet. Cover and simmer 2 minutes. Serve with rice or pasta. Serves 4.

ZUCCHINI BOATS

*4 small zucchini, 4-5 inches long
   or 2 large zucchini cut in half
Butter
Garlic salt*

*Dry bread crumbs
Parmesan cheese
Paprika*

Steam zucchini 8 minutes; cool under cold water. Cut in half lengthwise.
Spread with butter and sprinkle with salt, bread crumbs, Parmesan and
paprika. Bake about 6 minutes at 400°.

GREEK SALAD

*4 tomatoes, cut in wedges
2 cucumbers, sliced
2 green peppers, cut in strips*

*4 green onions, sliced
10 pitted black olives (Greek)
1/4 lb. feta cheese*

Layer vegetables and olives in large bowl. Crumble cheese on top. Chill
several hours. Pour dressing over just before serving.

Dressing:
*1/2 cup olive oil
1/4 cup red wine vinegar
1 clove garlic, minced*

*1/2 tsp. oregano
1/2 tsp. salt
Freshly ground pepper*

Combine in a jar and shake well.

WALNUT TARTS

Pastry:
*3 oz. cream cheese at room
   temperature*

*1/2 cup butter
1 cup flour*

Blend cream cheese and butter. Stir in flour. Chill 1 hour. Shape into 2
dozen 1-inch balls. Place in tiny ungreased muffin tins. Press dough on
bottom and sides of tins.

Walnut Filling:
*1 egg
3/4 cup brown sugar
1 Tbs. butter, softened
1 tsp. vanilla*

*Dash of salt
3/4 cup coarsely chopped walnuts,
   divided*

Beat egg, sugar, butter, vanilla and salt together. Place half of the nuts
in pastry cups. Add egg mixture and remaining nuts. Bake for 25
minutes at 325°. Cool and remove from tins.

Barbecued Pork Roast

Barley Casserole

Marinated Vegetables

Garlic Bread

Berry Ice Cream Topping

BARBECUED PORK ROAST

½ cup soy sauce
½ cup white wine
⅛ tsp. ginger
¼ tsp. mustard

¼ tsp. salt
1 clove garlic, minced
½ onion, chopped
3-4 lb. pork roast

Combine all ingredients and pour over roast. Cover and marinate all day, turning several times. Drain and cook roast in a covered barbecue. Allow 30 minutes per pound or until meat thermometer registers 170°. Brush occasionally with marinade. Strain marinade and serve hot with meat.

BARLEY CASSEROLE

4 Tbs. butter
¼ cup chopped green onion
¼ cup toasted slivered almonds
¼ cup chopped fresh parsley

2 cups chicken or beef broth
1 cup barley, rinsed and drained.
¼ tsp. salt

Saute onions in butter 3 minutes. Add almonds and parsley and mix. Add broth, barley and salt. Pour into buttered casserole and bake covered at 375° for 1 hour. Remove lid and bake 10 minutes longer. Serves 4-6.

MARINATED VEGETABLES

4-5 carrots, cut diagonally in
 ¼-inch slices
2 cups cauliflower flowerets
2 cups broccoli flowerets
1-2 zucchini, sliced in ½-inch
 pieces

1 cup cherry tomatoes, halved, or
 1 cut up tomato
1 onion, sliced
1 green pepper, cut in strips

Steam carrots 5 minutes. Add cauliflower, broccoli and zucchini and steam 5 minutes longer. Drain under cold water. Mix all vegetables together. Pour dressing over and stir. Chill 4 hours or overnight. Drain and serve.

Dressing:

½ cup salad oil
¼ cup white wine vinegar
1 Tbs. minced parsley
1 Tbs. grated onion

1 tsp. salt
¼ tsp. pepper
¾ tsp. dry mustard
½ tsp. chervil

Combine and mix well.

BERRY ICE CREAM TOPPING

1 pint strawberries, cut in half
¼ cup sugar
1 pkg. (10 oz.) frozen raspberries,
 thawed

2 Tbs. brandy
1 tsp. lemon juice

Mix strawberries with sugar. Blend frozen raspberries in food processor. Press through a strainer. Combine with brandy, lemon juice and strawberries. Serve over ice cream.

Cheese Wafers

Grilled Pork Chops

Corn on the Cob with Herb Butter

Marinated Tomato Slices

Peppers Saute

Apple-Oatmeal Squares

CHEESE WAFERS

*½ cup butter or margarine,
  softened
1 cup (4 oz.) shredded Cheddar
  cheese*

*1 cup flour
¼ tsp. Worcestershire sauce
¼ tsp. salt*

Cream butter and cheese. Stir in flour, Worcestershire and salt. Divide dough in half. Wrap in waxed paper. Chill 3 hours. Cut slices ⅛-¼ inch thick. Place on greased cookie sheets. Bake 10-12 minutes at 375°.

GRILLED PORK CHOPS

4-6 pork chops

Marinade:
*Juice of 1 lemon
¼ tsp. rosemary
¼ cup white wine*

*1 tsp. white wine vinegar
¼ tsp. salt
Pepper*

Marinate pork chops for 4 hours in marinade. Drain and grill 12-15 minutes turning several times.

CORN on the COB with HERB BUTTER

½ cup soft butter or margarine
*1 Tbs. each finely chopped parsley
and green onions*
*¼ tsp. each dry mustard and
fines herbes*

¼ tsp. garlic powder
*⅛ tsp. each salt and liquid hot
pepper seasoning*
Dash of freshly ground pepper

Combine and spread over ears of corn.

PEPPERS SAUTE

1 clove garlic, minced
¼ cup olive or vegetable oil
*3-4 large green peppers, seeded
and cut into squares*
2 medium onions, sliced

2 large tomatoes, cut in wedges
½ tsp. basil
½ tsp. salt

Saute garlic in oil for a few minutes. Add peppers and onions. Cook gently for 10 minutes, stirring occasionally. Add tomatoes, basil and salt. Cook until tender.

APPLE-OATMEAL SQUARES

1 cup flour
¾ tsp. baking soda
½ tsp. salt
½ tsp. allspice
½ cup oil
½ cup granulated sugar

½ cup brown sugar
1 egg
1 tsp. vanilla
1 cup rolled oats
1 cup finely chopped apples
½ cup chopped walnuts

Stir together flour, baking soda, salt and allspice. Combine oil, sugar, egg and vanilla; mix well. Add flour mixture and oats. Stir in apple and nuts. Spread in greased and floured 8-inch square baking pan. Bake at 350° for 35-40 minutes. Cut in squares and serve warm with ice cream.

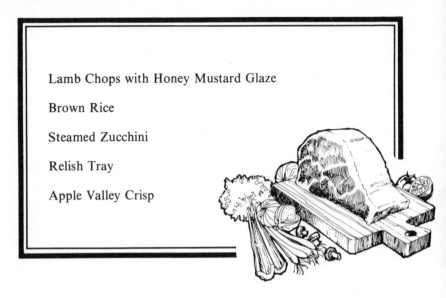

Lamb Chops with Honey Mustard Glaze

Brown Rice

Steamed Zucchini

Relish Tray

Apple Valley Crisp

LAMB CHOPS with HONEY-MUSTARD GLAZE

2 Tbs. Dijon mustard
¼ cup honey
1 tsp. soy sauce
1 clove garlic, minced

½ tsp. salt
¼ tsp. ginger
4 lamb chops, trimmed

Mix all ingredients except lamb chops. Arrange lamb chops on broiler 3-4 inches from heat. Spread half of the mustard glaze on top of each chop. Broil 6 minutes. Turn and brush with remaining glaze. Broil 6-7 minutes to desired doneness.

BROWN RICE

1 cup brown rice
2 cups water or vegetable broth
½ tsp. salt
1 Tbs. butter
1 Tbs. vegetable oil
½ onion, chopped
1 green pepper, chopped

2 ribs celery, diced
½ lb. mushrooms, sliced
¼ tsp. each sage, marjoram and
    thyme
1 Tbs. red wine vinegar
¼ cup minced parsley

Bring water or broth to boil. Stir in rice and salt. Cover and cook over low heat for 45 minutes. Saute onions, celery and green peppers in butter and oil until soft. Add mushrooms, sage, marjoram, thyme and wine vinegar; simmer over low heat for 10 minutes. Stir in parsley. Combine rice and mushroom mixture.

APPLE VALLEY CRISP

6 large apples
2 Tbs. lemon juice
½ tsp. cinnamon
½ cup white sugar
½ cup brown sugar

¾ cup flour
¼ tsp. salt
6 Tbs. butter
Ice cream

Peel and slice apples. Mix with juice. Mix cinnamon and white sugar and sprinkle over apples. Combine brown sugar, flour, salt and butter with pastry blender until mixture is crumbly. Spread over apples. Bake 40 minutes at 375°. Serve with ice cream.

Game

Game

Baked Pheasant

Wild Rice

Carrots in Wine

Tossed Salad

Baked Pears with Chocolate Sauce

Oregon Pinot Noir

BAKED PHEASANT

1 pheasant, quartered
¼ cup flour
1 tsp. salt
⅛ tsp. pepper
3 Tbs. butter
1 Tbs. oil
½ lb. mushrooms, sliced

3 green onions, sliced
½ cup chicken stock
½ cup white wine
¾ cup sour cream
Salt and pepper to taste
¼ cup chopped walnuts, optional

Dust pheasant in flour and seasonings. Brown in butter and oil. Place in Dutch oven or casserole. Saute mushrooms and onions. Add stock and wine and bring to a boil. Pour over pheasant. Cover and bake 1 hour at 350°. Remove pheasant to platter. Pour off excess fat. Stir sour cream into juices. Add salt and pepper. Return pheasant to pan and bake uncovered 30 minutes longer at 325°. Add walnuts if desired.

CARROTS in WINE

6 carrots, cut in thirds
½ cup white wine
½ tsp. fines herbes

¼ tsp. salt
⅛ tsp. white pepper
1 Tbs. butter

Cook carrots in wine and seasonings on low heat about 20 minutes. Add butter.

BAKED PEARS with CHOCOLATE SAUCE

3 pears, cut in half and cored   *Chopped nuts*
½ cup red wine

Place pears cut side down in baking dish. Add wine. Bake 15 minutes at
350°. Drain and serve with chocolate sauce. Sprinkle with nuts.

Chocolate Sauce:
1½ cups semi-sweet chocolate bits   *1 Tbs. strong coffee*
¼ cup cream   *Dash of cinnamon*
3 Tbs. red wine

Melt chocolate bits in cream, stirring constantly, add wine, coffee and
cinnamon. Serve warm.

Sauerkraut Duck

Oven Fried Potatoes

Orange-Cucumber Salad

French Bread

Cranberry Crunch

Washington Merlot

SAUERKRAUT DUCK

4 ducks (1 per person)
¼ cup butter, softened
Garlic salt
1 jar (1 pt., 6 oz.) sauerkraut,
drained

1 large onion, finely chopped
1 celery rib, finely chopped

Clean inside of ducks and drain. Dry with a towel. Mix butter with garlic salt and rub inside and out. Mix sauerkraut with onion and celery. Stuff each duck. Place in greased shallow pan and bake 35-40 minutes at 500°. Drain and wrap in foil for 10 minutes to keep warm and to finish cooking. Make sauce.

Sauce:
Drippings from pan
½-¾ cup catsup
2 drops Tabasco
1 Tbs. lemon juice

¼ cup soy sauce
1 Tbs. flour
¼ cup water

Mix drippings, catsup, Tabasco, lemon juice and soy sauce. Mix flour with water and add to sauce. Stir-cook until thickened.

Remove foil from ducks. Slit on both sides of breastbone. Place on warm platter and pour a small amount of sauce over. Pass remaining sauce.

OVEN FRIED POTATOES

4 potatoes, peeled   *½ tsp. salt*
¼ cup oil   *¼ tsp. paprika*

Cut potatoes into strips about ½ inch thick. Soak in cold water 10 minutes. Dry with paper towels. Spread in single layer in baking dish. Pour oil over and stir to coat. Bake 30 minutes at 500°. Turn several times. Drain on paper towels and sprinkle with salt, pepper and paprika. Serves 4.

ORANGE-CUCUMBER SALAD

3 large oranges, peeled and sliced   *1 onion, sliced*
1 cucumber, sliced   *Spinach leaves*

Arrange oranges, cucumber and onion slices alternately on spinach leaves. Pour on Poppy Seed Dressing (page 19).

CRANBERRY CRUNCH

1 cup uncooked rolled oats   *½ cup butter*
½ cup flour   *1 can (1 lb.) jellied cranberry sauce*
1 cup brown sugar

Mix oats, flour and sugar. Cut in butter until crumbly. Place half the mixture in an 8x8 greased baking dish. Cover with cranberry sauce. Top with remaining crumb mixture. Bake 45 minutes at 350°.

Game

Duck in Wine

Poppy Seed Noodles

Brussels Sprouts with Cheese Sauce

Fruit Plate

Warm Rolls

Apricot Bars

Oregon Pinot Noir

DUCK in WINE

3-4 ducks, skinned
½ cup flour
1 tsp. salt
¼ tsp. pepper
1 Tbs. oil

2-3 Tbs. butter
2 onions, chopped
2 stalks celery, chopped
1½ cups red wine

Cut off legs; remove breast and cut in two. Dredge in flour, salt and pepper. Brown legs and breast pieces in oil and butter. Place in pan and add onion, celery and wine. Cover and bake 2 hours at 300°. Serves 4.

POPPY SEED NOODLES

8 oz. noodles
1 Tbs. salt

¼ cup butter or margarine, melted
1 Tbs. poppy seed

Add noodles to boiling salted water. Cook 7-10 minutes. Stir with fork to prevent sticking. Drain in a colander. Do not rinse. Mix with butter and poppy seeds.

BRUSSELS SPROUTS with CHEESE SAUCE

1 lb. Brussels sprouts

Cut off stems. Soak in salted water 10 minutes. Drain and steam 10 minutes. Serve with Cheese Sauce.

Cheese Sauce:

2 Tbs. butter or margarine
2 Tbs. flour
1 cup milk or light cream
½ tsp. dry mustard

¾ tsp. salt
Dash pepper
1 cup grated sharp Cheddar cheese

Melt butter and blend in flour. Cook 1 minute. Add milk and seasonings. Bring to a boil stirring constantly. Reduce heat and stir in cheese until smooth.

APRICOT BARS

Crust:

1 cup butter
½ cup sugar

2 cups flour

Mix until crumbly. Pat in 9x13″ pan and bake 20 minutes at 350°.

Filling:

8 oz. dried apricots
⅔ cup flour
1 tsp. baking powder
½ tsp. salt

2 cups brown sugar
4 eggs, well beaten
1 tsp. vanilla
1 cup chopped nuts

Cover apricots with water and boil 10 minutes. Puree apricots and juice in food processor. Set aside to cool. Sift flour, baking powder and salt together. Beat sugar into eggs. Add dry ingredients. Add apricots and nuts. Spread filling over crust and bake 30 minutes longer. Cool and frost with Cream Cheese Frosting (page 87). Use ½ of the recipe. Cut in squares.

Game

Hunter's Swiss Steak

Rice or Noodles

Cauliflower with Egg Topping

Fall Fruit Salad

Fresh Pear Pie

Oregon or Washington
   Cabernet Sauvignon

HUNTER'S SWISS STEAK

1½-2 lbs. venison round steak, cut
   1½ inches thick
Flour
½ tsp. salt
¼ tsp. pepper
3 Tbs. oil

2 large onions, chopped
1 celery rib, chopped
1½ cups whole tomatoes
2 Tbs. Worcestershire sauce
2 tsp. cornstarch
2 Tbs. water

Dredge meat with flour seasoned with salt and pepper. Brown on all sides in oil. Add vegetables and Worcestershire. Cover tightly and cook 1½ hours or until very tender. Remove meat and thicken gravy with cornstarch mixed with water. Stir-cook until smooth and blended.

CAULIFLOWER with EGG TOPPING

1 large head cauliflower

Cut cauliflower into flowerets and cook in boiling salted water 15 minutes or until tender. Drain. Spoon on topping and serve immediately.

Topping:
½ cup finely chopped onion   *3 Tbs. chopped parsley*
3 Tbs. butter   *Salt and pepper to taste*
2 hard-cooked eggs, chopped   *Dash garlic salt*
2 Tbs. fine bread crumbs

Saute onion in butter. Add remaining ingredients.

FALL FRUIT SALAD

Apples   *Grapes*
Raisins   *Nuts*
Bananas

Cut or chop to desired size and toss with dressing.

Dressing:
1 cup sour cream or yogurt   *3-4 Tbs. pineapple juice*
½ cup grated Cheddar cheese

Combine and mix well.

FRESH PEAR PIE

6-7 pears, halved and peeled   *4 Tbs. flour*
Unbaked pastry shell   *2 eggs*
1 cup sugar   *1 tsp. vanilla*
¼ cup butter

Place pears in pastry shell. Mix remaining ingredients and pour over pears. Bake 40-45 minutes at 325°.

Game

Venison Sauerbraten

Potato Pancakes

Beets with Sour Cream

Coleslaw

Apple Cake

Oregon Pinot Noir

VENISON SAUERBRATEN

2 lbs. chuck or rump roast of
   venison
1 cup vinegar
6 peppercorns
5 whole cloves
2 bay leaves
½ tsp. salt

3 Tbs. fat
6 carrots
2 onions
1 cup sliced celery
1 Tbs. sugar
10 gingersnaps, crushed

Trim all fat from venison. Place in a glass dish. Add the next 5 ingredients. Add water to cover. Cover and refrigerate for at least 5 days. Turn several times. Remove from marinade and reserve liquid for gravy. Brown meat on all sides in fat. Add vegetables and 2 cups of marinade. Cover and simmer until meat and vegetables are tender (1½-1¾ hours). Remove meat and vegetables from pan. Add sugar and gingersnaps to make gravy. Serve with meat and vegetables.

POTATO PANCAKES

4 potatoes, coarsely grated
1/4 cup onion, grated
2 eggs, slightly beaten
2 Tbs. flour

1/2 tsp. salt
Dash each of pepper and
 nutmeg
Oil for frying

Combine all ingredients except oil. Heat oil 1/8-inch deep in large skillet. For each pancake, drop 2 Tbs. potato mixture into hot fat. Flatten down with a turner to 4 inches diameter. Fry 2-3 minutes on each side. Drain on paper towel. Keep warm in the oven. Will make 10-12 pancakes.

BEETS with SOUR CREAM SAUCE

2 dozen very small beets

Cut off tops and wash. Steam 30-40 minutes until tender. Drain. Run under cold water and slip off skins. Serve with Sour Cream Sauce.

Sour Cream Sauce:

1/2 cup sour cream
1 tsp. horseradish
1 tsp. lemon juice

1/4 tsp. salt
1/4 tsp. pepper

Combine and mix well.

APPLE CAKE

1/4 cup butter
1 cup sugar
1 egg
1/2 tsp. cinnamon
1/2 tsp. nutmeg
1 tsp. baking soda

1/4 tsp. salt
1 cup sifted flour
2 cups diced apples
1/2 cup chopped nuts
1 tsp. vanilla

Cream butter and sugar. Add egg and mix well. Sift dry ingredients together and add to creamed mixture. Stir in apples, nuts and vanilla. Bake in a greased 9x9 baking dish for 40-45 minutes at 350°. Serve warm or cold with Buttery-Sweet Sauce if desired.

Buttery-Sweet Sauce:

1 cup sugar
1/2 cup butter

1/2 cup light cream
1/4 tsp. vanilla or rum flavoring

Combine ingredients and heat. Serve warm.

Game

Barbecued Venison Chops

Wild or Brown Rice

Stir-Fry Broccoli and Mushrooms
    with Almonds

Salad Greens with Avocado Dressing

Popovers

Plum Cobbler

Oregon Pinot Noir

BARBECUED VENISON CHOPS

2 venison chops per person　　*1 tsp. chili powder*
½ cup olive oil　　*1 tsp. salt*
2 cloves garlic, chopped　　*2 dashes Tabasco*
1 cup catsup　　*⅓ cup water*
1 Tbs. Worcestershire sauce

Marinate chops 4 hours in olive oil and garlic. Drain and place in baking dish and add 4 Tbs. marinating oil. Bake uncovered 15 minutes at 400°. Make sauce of remaining ingredients and pour over chops. Cover and bake 1½ hours at 325°.

WILD or BROWN RICE

1 cup wild or brown rice　　*1 tsp. salt*
3 cups chicken broth　　*2 Tbs. butter*

Drain wild rice under hot water (omit if using brown rice). Place in a pan with broth and bring to a boil. Reduce heat; cover and simmer 50-60 minutes. Add butter.

STIR-FRY BROCCOLI and MUSHROOMS
with ALMONDS

1 bunch broccoli (about 1¾ lbs.),
   trimmed and divided into
   spears
6-8 mushrooms, sliced
3 Tbs. oil
1 clove garlic, split

½ tsp. salt
2 Tbs. lemon juice
2 Tbs. slivered almonds

Saute garlic in oil 1 minute. Remove garlic. Add broccoli and mushrooms and stir-fry about 3 minutes. Add ½ cup water. Cover and steam 5 minutes. Drain. Add salt, lemon juice and almonds. Toss and serve.

AVOCADO DRESSING

1 avocado, cut up
½ cup sour cream
½ cup mayonnaise
3 Tbs. white wine vinegar
1 clove garlic
2 parsley sprigs

1 tsp. Worcestershire sauce
¼ tsp. tarragon
½ tsp. salt
½ tsp. mustard
⅛ tsp. pepper

Place all ingredients in food processor or blender. Blend until smooth. Serve on salad greens.

POPOVERS

4 eggs
1⅓ cups flour
1⅓ cups milk

¼ tsp. salt
1 Tbs. salad oil

Place all ingredients in blender. Blend well, scraping down the sides as necessary. Pour into 12 greased muffin cups and bake 35-40 minutes at 375°.

Game

PLUM COBBLER

3 lbs. purple plums
²/₃ cup sugar
½ tsp. EACH cinnamon and salt

¼ tsp. nutmeg
Ice Cream

Halve and pit plums. Place cut side down in 2 layers in a buttered 9x13 baking pan. Combine sugar, cinnamon, salt and nutmeg and sprinkle over plums. Bake uncovered for 20 minutes at 350°. Cover with topping and bake 35 minutes longer. Serve with ice cream.

Topping:

1½ cups all-purpose flour
2 tsp. baking powder
½ cup sugar
¼ tsp. salt
2 eggs, slightly beaten

¾ cup milk
1 tsp. vanilla
¼ cup butter, melted
¾ cup chopped walnuts
1 Tbs. sugar

Mix first 4 ingredients together and combine with eggs, milk, vanilla, and butter. Pour over plum mixture. Sprinkle nuts and sugar on top.

Index

142